The Stamp Act
and the
American Revolution

Journal of the American Revolution Books highlight the latest research on new or lesser-known topics of the revolutionary era. The *Journal of the American Revolution* is an online resource and annual volume that provides educational, peer-reviewed articles by professional historians and experts in American Revolution studies.

Also by Ken Shumate in the Series

1764: *The First Year of the American Revolution*

The Sugar Act and the American Revolution

A JOURNAL OF THE AMERICAN REVOLUTION BOOK

THE STAMP ACT
AND THE
AMERICAN REVOLUTION

KEN SHUMATE

WESTHOLME
Yardley

Westholme Publishing, LLC
904 Edgewood Road
Yardley, Pennsylvania 19067
Visit our Web site at www.westholmepublishing.com

ISBN: 978-1-59416-460-6
Also available as an eBook.

Printed in the United States of America.

CONTENTS

PREFACE

> What do We mean by the American Revolution? Do We mean the American War? The Revolution was effected before the War commenced. The Revolution was in the Minds and Hearts of the People.
>
> —John Adams, 1818

Historian Joseph Ellis has pointed out that following the British victory in the Seven Years' War a new imperial policy began in 1763 with a proclamation from George III preventing westward expansion beyond the Appalachian Mountains. "The next installment of the new imperial policy came in the form of three acts of Parliament: the Sugar Act (1764), Stamp Act (1765), and Townshend Acts (1767)." This book deals with the second of those three acts of Parliament.[1]

The Stamp Act of 1765 was a tax levied on colonists in the British North American colonies in the same manner that Parliament taxed British subjects in England, Wales, and Scotland. The intent of Parliament to levy such a tax was announced in 1764. The colonies protested late that year based on a constitutional issue, that the unrepresented colonies could not be taxed by Parliament. It is "the undoubted Right of Englishmen, that no Taxes be imposed on them, but with their own Consent, given personally, or by their Representatives."[2] Parliament not only rejected the colonial petitions but—outraged by them—passed the Stamp Act in early 1765 as affirmation of the sovereignty of Parliament.

The colonies denied the right of Parliament to impose such a tax, and then violently resisted its implementation, leading Parliament to repeal the act in 1766. The taxation and resulting colonial resistance resulted in a political great awakening. "The Stamp Act crisis . . . stirred Americans as nothing before in their history. It produced a fundamental clarification of the American conception of the constitutional relationship that should exist between the colonies and Great Britain."[3]

My intent is to provide insight into the Stamp Act: why British leaders thought the tax was necessary; why the plan to enact it was announced in 1764; why and how Americans protested against it later that year; how it was enacted in 1765; how it was vigorously resisted in every colony; and why and how it was repealed in 1766. Although there are many aspects to the controversy, I focus on taxation both when describing the nature and effect of the Stamp Act and when describing American protests. "It was direct parliamentary taxation of the colonies after 1763 that began the final dispute between Britain and the American colonies." In a more colorful phrase, "Taxation was to be the anvil on which the Anglo-American relationship broke."[4]

In telling this story I follow the strategy suggested by John Adams. "The records of the British government, and the records of all the thirteen colonies, and the pamphlets, newspapers, and handbills of both parties must be examined, and the essence extracted, before a correct history can be written of the American Revolution."[5] That the records of both parties be considered is necessary in order to describe how action on one side of the Atlantic Ocean affected response on the other. I rely upon contemporary writing to tell the story, letting the actors speak in their own words, showing mood, spirit, and attitude as part of the speech, essay, letter, pamphlet, or report. I annotate extracts from statutes, petitions, resolves, pamphlets, letters, essays, parliamentary debates, and other official documents, using the original text to dramatize time and place. For clarity, I do occasionally modernize the original text, but more often retain the original, sometimes awkward and inconsistent, spelling and punctuation. Quotations from conversations or speeches are usually the literal words of that person but are sometimes reports or summaries (e.g., parliamentary histories based on diaries or letters), not the exact words of the speaker. I will occasionally highlight certain phrases (*in italic*) in order to stress their importance or to call attention to related contemporary writings.

The structure of the book is event-based and primarily chronological, driven by the back-and-forth nature of unfolding events. Part One addresses the events and thinking in Great Britain that led to the Sugar Act of 1764 and the announcement of the intent to impose stamp duties; those British actions prompted American protests late that year. Such petitions and other writings angered British officials, making for smooth passage of the Stamp Act in 1765. Part Two describes different aspects of American resistance: a congress of colonies to declare a consensus constitutional stance on taxation, a boycott of British products, and a refusal to allow the act to take effect. Part Three is devoted to British retreat: the backlash to colonial resistance, parliamentary debate regarding the choice between enforcement and conciliation, and ending with repeal of the Stamp Act.

Showing how the British reacted to the boycott and the nullification of the act, and how they interpreted the objections made by the Americans, provides insight into decisions made by British leaders in the following decade.

PROLOGUE

The British Stamp Act of 1694

IN 1694, Parliament passed "An Act for granting to their Majesties several duties upon vellum, parchment and paper, for four years, towards carrying on the war against France."[1] Duties were to be paid on the use of documents such as diplomas from colleges, deeds, licenses for sale of wine or spirits, and most sorts of papers used in courts of law. The method for collecting the tax was based on revenue stamps (stamps showing the amount of the tax). Taxed documents were required to be created on writing material that was sold by the British Stamp Office, such material bearing a stamp showing the tax had been paid. The requirement to use stamped paper led to the taxation law being popularly referred to as a *Stamp Act.*

This proclamation of May 1694, "Given at Our Court in Whitehall . . . In the sixth Year of Our Reign" put the act into effect.

> By the King and Queen
> A PROCLAMATION
> For Publishing the several Marks or Stamps to be used for Vellum, Parchment and Paper, pursuant to a late Act of Parliament for Charging certain Duties thereupon.
>
> Whereas in and by an Act . . . [stamp commissioners will provide for] Marks or Stamps, to Stamp or Impress all Velum, Parchment and Paper, upon which any Records, Deeds, Instru-

> ments, Writings, Copies, or other things by the said Act charged, may be Ingrossed or Written, That is to say . . .

The proclamation then goes on to list six rates of duty and the documents to be stamped and charged at each rate. Here is a summary of the lengthy list.

> Duty 1d: Pleadings in the Law Courts, copies of wills, formal depositions.
> Duty 6d: Certain affidavits, leases, a great variety of writs.
> Duty 1s: Certain summonses, certificates of matriculation from Oxford & Cambridge Universities.
> Duty 2s6d: A variety of legal documents.
> Duty 5s: Deeds relating to fines, marriage certificates, probates of wills, appeals and sentences in the Courts of Admiralty.
> Duty 40s: Royal grants of any honour, promotion, pardon or land. Presentation to ecclesiastical benefices, certificates of degrees of the Universities or Inns of Court.

The stamp duties imposed for four years under the 1694 Act proved so profitable and so easy to collect that at the end of that period they were made perpetual and later extended to Scotland.

Over time, additional taxes were levied. Shipping debentures paid eight pence; bills of lading fourpence; licenses for retailing wine four shillings per annum, for beer and ale one shilling, for spirituous liquors one pound; for cards sixpence a pack and dice five shillings a pair, and more:

> The following duties were imposed on books, newspapers, pamphlets, and advertisements: (i) every paper containing a half-sheet of paper or less, a halfpenny; (ii) every paper containing a whole sheet of paper, one penny; (iii) above one sheet . . . to pay at the rate of two shillings per sheet; advertisements in the *London Gazette* or any other "public weekly" to bear a shilling stamp. The paper duty was not to extend to published acts of parliament, proclamations, votes of the house of com-

mons, or to any book "commonly used in schools . . . or containing only matters of devotion or piety."[2]

PART ONE

Taxation

"The sad story of colonial oppression commenced in the year 1764. Great Britain then adopted new regulations respecting her colonies, which, after disturbing the ancient harmony of the two countries for about twelve years, terminated in a dismemberment of the empire."

—David Ramsay, 1789

One

Revenue

"Towards defraying the necessary Expences of defending, protecting and securing the British Colonies and Plantations in America, it may be proper to charge certain Stamp Duties in the said Colonies and Plantations."

—Secretary of State Halifax, August 1764

THE END OF THE SEVEN YEARS' WAR led to profound changes in the relationship between Great Britain and the British colonies in North America. Victorious Great Britain in 1763 was ceded extensive territory by France and Spain. In order to secure the new territory, British leaders decided to retain in the colonies a large peacetime garrison: regiments of the British Regular Army. In order to not further burden British taxpayers already paying heavy taxes to support the debt resulting from the war, it was necessary that the colonies provide financial support for those troops. In 1764, Parliament passed legislation assessing a large number of customs duties intended to provide a portion of the needed revenue. The law is now commonly referred to as the *Sugar Act of 1764*. Important to the Stamp Act story is that Parliament at the same time announced an intent to levy stamp duties in the colonies, duties similar to those in Great Britain.

Planning Taxation

On May 30, 1763, a letter of March 27 from London was published in the Rhode Island *Newport Mercury*. It describes the planning for taxes to be levied on the colonies. The writer reports

> a matter much the subject of conversation here, which, if carried into execution, will, in its consequences, greatly affect the colonies. It is the quartering sixteen regiments in America, to be supported at the expense of the Provinces. . . . The money, it is said, will be levied by act of parliament, and arise on a Stamp duty, excise on rum distilled on the continent, and a duty on *foreign sugar and molasses* etc., by reducing the former duty on these last mentioned articles, which it is found impracticable to collect, to such a one as will be collected.

The "former duty" had been imposed by an act of 1733 often called the *Molasses Act*. The duties on foreign sugar and molasses had as their purpose the regulation of trade, there being no duty charged on imports from British colonies in the West Indies. Particularly onerous was the duty on molasses, important for distillation into rum. The duties were indeed impracticable to collect: colonial merchants evaded them by smuggling and bribing of customs officials.

> This manner of raising money, except what may arise on the foreign sugars, &c., I apprehend, will be thought greatly to diminish even the appearance of the subject's liberty, since nothing seems to be more repugnant to the general principles of freedom than the subjecting a people to taxation by laws in the enactment of which they are not represented.[1]

The story begins in April 1763 when George Grenville became first minister, that is, head of the government as first lord of the treasury and chancellor of the exchequer. It became his responsibility to enact the legislation necessary to raise revenue from the colonies. The changes he put into place have become known as the Grenville program, a shortcut phrase for the Grenville ministry's American legislation of 1763–1765. In addition to the need to raise revenue for the peacetime garrison, Grenville needed to deal with the broader problem: the American colonies were drifting away from what was perceived as a necessary subservience to the mother country.[2] Grenville's first move was to require strict compliance with the laws of trade (i.e., "Acts of Trade and Navigation" or the "Navigation Act"). Another was to renew the soon-to-expire Molasses Act, at the same time making changes to increase the revenue. However, since such a source of revenue was limited ("custom duties had a bound," Grenville said) it was necessary to look for additional sources of funding.

On July 5, Henry McCulloh, a British official previously stationed in America, suggested a mechanism for additional revenue: stamp duties such as those long in use in Great Britain. This was only the latest in a long line of eighteenth-century recommendations that stamp duties be used to raise revenue in the colonies.

> A stamp duty on vellum and paper in America, at sixpence, twelve pence, and eighteen pence per sheet, would, at a moderate computation, amount to upwards of sixty thousand sterling per annum, or, if extended to the West Indies, would produce double that sum.

McCulloh included a draft bill: *Proposals with respect to a Stamp Duty on America.* Grenville soon became convinced of the value of such duties, and in September ordered preparation of a bill defining stamp duties to be levied.[3]

By late September Grenville had settled on his plan to renew and revise the act of 1733: reduce the unenforceable ("impracticable to collect") molasses duty, place duties on additional imported products, appropriate the revenue to British forces in America, and establish regulations facilitating enforcement of the laws of trade. He sent a lengthy report to the Privy Council on October 4. This report is important, even famous, as it provided the basis for many provisions of the Sugar Act of 1764. The report also deals with Britain's broader problem with the colonies.

> Their vast Increase in Territory and Population makes the proper Regulation of their Trade of immediate Necessity, lest the continuance and extent of the dangerous Evils . . . may render all Attempts to remedy them hereafter infinitely more difficult, if not utterly impracticable.

On October 5, the Privy Council issued an order stating acceptance of the plan.[4]

Disruption of American Trade

On June 21, 1763, in accordance with a recent law that had the effect of empowering officers of the British navy to act as customs officials, the lords of the Admiralty wrote commanders of ships in the American fleet, ordering them to "seize and proceed to condemnation of all such Ships and Vessels as you shall find offending against the said laws."[5]

On July 9, the secretary of state directed the colonial governors "to put an effectual Stop to the clandestine Running of Goods into any place within your Jurisdiction."

> The King wishes that all possible Means should be used to root out so iniquitous a Practice; a Practice carried on in Contravention of many express & repeated Laws, [leading] to the Diminution & Impoverishment of the Public Revenue.[6]

By late 1763, the enforcement actions were having a troublesome effect on American commerce. Massachusetts governor Francis Bernard wrote his friend Richard Jackson on November 26: "The Merchants here are greatly alarmed at the present proceedings to guard this Coast & especially the appointing the Captains of the men of War to be Customhouse Officers."[7] Richard Jackson was an important player in the Stamp Act story. He was not only a friend to Bernard, he was London agent for Connecticut and Pennsylvania and soon to become a Massachusetts agent as well. Jackson was widely respected, a member of the House of Commons, and had a close relationship with Grenville. Bernard wrote Jackson again on January

7, 1764: "The publication of orders for the strict execution of the Melasses Act has caused a [great] alarm in this Country . . . the Merchants say, there is an end of the trade of this Province."[8]

In early 1764, three colonies protested against the strict enforcement of the laws of trade and the intent to renew the Molasses Act. Rhode Island governor Stephen Hopkins published in the Providence *Gazette* of January 14 *An Essay on the Trade of the Northern Colonies of Great Britain in North America*, describing the harmful effect of the duties expected to be imposed by the renewal.[9] "The commerce of the British northern colonies in America is [made difficult because] the soil and climate of them is incapable of producing almost anything which will serve to send directly home to the mother country." In consequence, the purchase of British products is possible only because exports are "sold for money or bills of exchange, which are sent directly to England."

In addition to the essay, the "Governor and Company" of Rhode Island on January 24 submitted a remonstrance "to the Right Honorable the Lords Commissioners for Trade and Plantations" that made it clear the most important product imported was molasses. The remonstrance points out that the result of trade with foreign islands was the "import into this colony about fourteen thousand hogsheads of molasses." Molasses was central to the economy of the colony: profit from exportation of the resulting rum "serves as an engine in the hands of the merchant to effect the great purpose of paying for British manufactures." Imports of British goods annually "amount at least to £120,000 sterling," while exports of "articles produced in the colony suitable for a remittance to Europe [amount only] to about £5,000 sterling, per annum."

> The present price of molasses is about twelve pence, sterling, per gallon; at which rate, only, it can be distilled into rum for exportation; wherefore, if a duty should be laid on this article, the enhanced price may amount to a prohibition; and it may with truth be said, that there is not so large a sum of silver and gold circulating in the colony, as the duty imposed by the aforesaid act upon foreign molasses, would amount to in one year, which makes it absolutely impossible for the importers to pay it.[10]

Although this makes it appear as though any molasses duty at all would prevent the profitable trade, the evolving American position was that one penny per gallon was reasonable—that being approximately the cost incurred to illegally import foreign molasses—and that twopence might be acceptable.

Protests were also submitted by Massachusetts and New York. None of the protests made an argument that the duties were beyond the authority of Parliament (all the colonies broadly accepting the validity of the Navigation Act), only that they were detrimental to the economy of the northern colonies—and ultimately damaging to the British economy as well. As it turned out, these protests had no influence on the nature of the Sugar Act.

Internal Taxation

At the same time that the three protests were being developed, the notion of *internal* taxation began to be raised (internal implying domestic matters, those affecting the internal activity of a colony). The distinction, in contrast to *external* taxation, plays a role throughout the story of the Stamp Act. It becomes part of the story in letters from Richard Jackson. On December 27, 1763, he wrote Benjamin Franklin, then a member of the Pennsylvania Committee of Correspondence.

> A Revenue to be raised in America for the Support of British Troops is not now to [be] argued against: it would answer no Purpose to do so. . . . It is not disputed that [each mother country] is Mistress of the Trade of its Colonys: this Right has always been . . . exercised by England and all other Countries; [since the mother country] may prohibit foreign Trade, it may therefore tax it. And the Colonys have a Compensation in Protection, *but I dread internal Taxes.*[11]

Jackson wrote again only a month later: "I have long since given up all hopes of preventing some Parliamentary Tax to be imposed on N America as well as the W Indies for the maintenance of the Troops kept there." He expresses concern for the form of taxation: "I am most averse to an Internal Tax, God knows how far such a precedent may be extended, and I have frequently asked, what internal Tax they will not lay." He explains what sort of taxation would be acceptable: "Customs as well as Prohibitions on Trade, have been at all times, laid by England. . . . I wish this to be the Rule of Conduct on this Occasion."[12]

THE GRENVILLE BUDGET

When Parliament opened on November 15, 1763, the king's speech called for attention to "the heavy debts contracted in the course of the late war." He called for both frugality and "the improvement of the public revenue, by such regulations as shall be judged most expedient for that purpose."[13] On March 9, 1764, Grenville presented to the Committee of Ways and Means (a committee of the whole house) his proposals for the improvement of the public revenue. He established a political reason for taxing the colonies: "We have expended much in America. Let us now avail ourselves of the fruits of that expense." As part of his discussion of the planned customs duties, he discussed the amount of revenue but admitted that "he cannot form any certain estimate: perhaps £40, 50 or 60,000."[14] Regarding the cost of the planned British regular troops in the colonies, "Expense of maintaining 10,000 in North America, amount £359,000." Grenville expressed his concern with the amount of the resulting revenue.

> He added that custom duties had a bound. Something farther must be thought of. A stamp duty in America twas easily collected, without a large body of officers. Britain has an inherent right to lay inland duties there. *The very sovereignty of this kingdom depends on it.*

The related resolve was the soon-to-be controversial and eventually infamous fifteenth resolution: *towards further defraying the said Expences, it may be proper to charge certain Stamp Duties in the said Colonies and Plantations.*

At this point, having heard rumblings "out of doors" to the contrary, Grenville wished to affirm that Parliament held the authority to impose an internal (inland) tax on America. He is convinced that America has the right to impose an inland tax: "If any man doubts the right of this country, he will take the opinion of the committee immediately." No man doubted, placing the House of Commons on the record as having the authority to levy an internal tax on the colonies.

Grenville ends with an obscure statement that hints at a possible alternative to the imposition of internal taxes by Parliament: "He would likewise wish to follow to a certain degree the inclination of the people in North America if they will agree to the end." Some colonies, based on reports from their agents thought that Grenville was open to the colonies taxing themselves and began to plan for such an event. Such efforts came to nought however and had little effect on the following course of the controversy.

In the mild debate following Grenville's presentation, John Huske who was born in New Hampshire but had resided in England for twenty-five years, had much to say. He supported the planned taxation but would involve the colonies before doing so.

> No doubt can exist of the right to tax North America in England. We [Americans] know we are subject to the legislature of this country. . . . Notice ought to be sent to North America of any important business which relates to them. . . . Would have this law read two times, printed and then sent to America for their opinion about it.

Other speakers supported Huske in the postponement of stamp duties. Grenville responded to the desire for delay: "As to stamp duty, desired it might be done with good will. That for the present session it might go no farther than a resolution." The postponement is of interest to our story since it allowed time for American objections to fester, grow, and be expressed later in 1764.[15] Although there was modest debate on the level of duty, there was no opposition to the bill.

On March 10, the committee of ways and means reported Grenville's resolutions to the full House of Commons, all eventually approved. They include, "[15] That, towards further defraying the said Expences, it may be proper to charge certain Stamp Duties in the said Colonies and Plantations." It was ordered "that a Bill, or Bills, be brought in pursuant to [all resolutions save the fifteenth]."

News to the Colonies

On December 30, 1763, Massachusetts agent Jasper Mauduit reported the status of the budget discussions. It was clear that "a practicable duty should be laid, and the payment of it enforced. To attempt to controvert either of these would be to no manner of purpose." He describes his situation.

> As the General Court have not been pleased to instruct me in their sentiments upon this subject, I was left to pursue my own. . . . And their silence inclined me to think that such a scheme, if duly moderated, might not be disagreeable, tho' they might not choose to appear openly to approve it.[16]

We will soon see that he misread the silence of the General Court.

On March 13, 1764, Mauduit reported Grenville's plan that the stamp duties were to be deferred until the next session of Parliament, "desirous, as [Grenville] expressed himself, to consult the Ease, the Quiet, and the Goodwill of the Colonies."[17]

Virginia agent Edward Montague on April 11 reported that

> the 15th resolution is the most alarming to the Colonies. [Grenville] hoped that the power & sovereignty of parliament over every part of the British dominions for the purpose of raising or collecting any tax would never be disputed. That if there was a single man doubted it, he would take the sense of the House, having heard without doors hints of this nature dropped.

Montague sees a hidden reason for Grenville's postponement of stamp duties: "He then called for the sense of Parliament, and *that the House might not suffer objections of that Nature at a future day.*" Not only was there no dissent, but

> the Members interested in the Plantations expressed great surprise that a doubt of that nature could ever exist. . . . The house appeared so unanimous of opinion that America should ease the revenue of this annual expense that I am perswaded they will not listen to any remonstrance against it.[18]

News of Grenville's March budget presentation quickly became widely known in the colonies. The *Pennsylvania Gazette* of May 10 published this report.

> Our other Advices by the Packet are, that a Scheme of Taxation of the American Colonies has for some Time been in Agitation: That it had been previously debated in Parliament, whether they had Power to lay such a Tax on Colonies which had no Representatives in Parliament, and determined in the Affirmative.
>
> That on the Ninth of March, Mr. [Grenville] made a long Harrangue on the melancholy State of the Nation, overloaded with heavy Taxes, and a Debt of £146 Millions, £52 Millions of which had arisen in the four last Years: That by a Computation, which he laid before the House, £360,000 Sterling per Annum was expended on North-America, and therefore it was but reasonable they should support the Troops sent out for their Defence, and all the other particular Expence of the Nation on their Account.

The article went on at length that money would be raised by the levy of duties on imported goods, then opened a new issue.

> Besides this, an internal Tax was proposed, a Stamp Duty, &c. but many Members warmly opposing it, this was deferred till next Session; but it was feared that the Tax upon foreign Goods would pass into a Law this Session.[19]

Acts of 1764

Parliament went on to pass the Sugar Act of 1764, receiving the royal assent on April 5.[20] The title of the act states that duties were to be imposed on imported goods for the purpose of "defraying the expences of defending, protecting, and securing" the colonies. The preamble addresses regulation of trade, "extending and securing the navigation and commerce" between Britain and the colonies, and is also explicit about "improving the revenue of this kingdom." Further, it makes positive affirmation that "it is just and necessary that a revenue be raised." In order to do so,

> we, your Majesty's most dutiful and loyal subjects, the commons of Great Britain . . . have resolved to give and grant unto your Majesty the several rates and duties herein-after-mentioned.

The words of art "give and grant" indicate that the duties collected were a gift of the commons of Great Britain: a tax. However, the nature of the act (being a revision of the trade regulation of 1733) led to its not being immediately recognized by the legislatures of most colonies as taxation.

The Sugar Act contained an additional objectionable feature: the expansion of jurisdiction of courts of admiralty and consequent denial of the right of trial by jury. The laws were to be enforced through use of either common-law courts "or in any court of admiralty . . . at the election of the informer or prosecutor." Admiralty courts had been traditionally limited to offenses on the high seas and below the first bridge on navigable rivers. In these courts, the judge ruled not only on matters of law but also on matters of fact—the role of juries in common-law courts.[21]

The Sugar Act became a grievance of the Americans; the colonial protests of 1764 and 1765 often combined Sugar Act and Stamp Act protests, making constitutional objections to the use of stamp duties and economic objections to the duties of the Sugar Act.

Following on the heels of the Sugar Act, Parliament passed "An Act to prevent paper bills of credit [in the colonies] from being declared to be a legal tender in payments of money." It received the royal assent on April 19 and is often called the Currency Act.[22] The act was another American grievance as it limited a necessary medium of exchange for business transactions, especially since the Sugar Act and later the Stamp Act demanded payment in British sterling money (leading to the "want of specie" or "hard currency"). The problem was often raised along with Sugar and Stamp Act protests.

Agents Meet with Grenville

The statement on March 9 by Grenville that he would "wish to follow . . . the inclination of the people in North America" combined with the postponement of stamp duties puzzled the colonial agents. Some reported that Grenville had implied he would not impose stamp duties if the colonies were to provide additional revenue to Great Britain by taxing themselves. The agents met to discuss the issue, deciding to request a meeting with Grenville. He granted an audience for May 17. Jasper Mauduit reported the meeting in a letter of May 26. "A few days ago, several of the Agents waited upon Mr. Grenville to know his intentions upon [stamp duties]."

> That of the several Inland duties, that of stamps was the most equal, & required the fewest officers, and was attended with the least Expence in the Collecting of it. That therefore, tho' he doubted not but that the Colonies would wish rather to have no tax at all; yet as the necessities of Government render'd it an indispensable duty, he should certainly bring in such a Bill, and in the meantime he should leave it to each province to signify their Assent to such a Bill in General.

When Grenville was asked about specifics of the bill (without which "it would be asking the province to assent to they did not know what") he "answered that that was not necessary. That everyone knew the stamp laws here; and that this Bill is intended to be formed upon the same plan."[23] Although the agents left unenlightened, they understood Grenville was committed to a bill for stamp duties.

Preparation of the Stamp Act

Thomas Whately (a secretary of the treasury and a particularly close confidante and spokesman for Grenville) in early April was assigned responsibility for preparation of a stamp bill. Whately wrote late that month to his friend Jared Ingersoll (an important Connecticut lawyer, influential statesman, and later agent). Whately referred to the taxes levied by the Sugar Act ("certainly these will not be sufficient to defray that Share of ye American Expence which America ought & is able to bear") then moves to the issue of stamp duties.

> A Stamp Act has been proposed. Would it yield a considerable Revenue if the Duty were low upon mercantile Instruments, high upon gratuitous Grants of Lands, & moderate upon Law Proceedings? Would ye Execution of such a Law be attended with great Inconveniencies, or open to frequent Evasions which could not be guarded against?[24]

Ingersoll received the letter on July 4, responding on July 6 with a warning about taxation.

> What shall I Answer to your queries relative to the proposed internal taxation of America? You say America can & ought to Contribute to its own defence; we one & all say ye same on this Side ye water—we only differ about the means.

The Americans would accept the usual procedure of requisitions but feared the precedent of the tax.

> If the King should fix the proportion of our Duty, we all say we will do our parts in ye Common Cause, but if the Parliament once interpose & Lay a tax, tho' it may be a very moderate one . . . what Consequences may, or rather may not, follow?

He warns of the difficulty of collecting a tax that violates constitutional rights.

> The people's minds not only here but in the neighbouring Provinces are filled with the most dreadfull apprehensions from such a Step's taking place, from whence I leave you to guess how Easily a tax of that kind would be Collected; tis difficult

> to say how many ways could be invented to avoid the payment of a tax laid upon a Country without the Consent of the Legislature of that Country & in the opinion of most of the people Contrary to the foundation principles of their natural & Constitutional rights & Liberties.

Any tax "other than such as shall be laid by the Legislative bodies here . . . would go down with the people like Chopt hay."[25]

On August 11, Secretary of State Halifax directed colonial governors to provide information necessary to further develop the bill. In addition, the letter served as official notification that stamp duties were to be imposed.

> Towards defraying the necessary Expences of defending, protecting and securing the British Colonies and Plantations in America, it may be proper to charge certain Stamp Duties in the said Colonies and Plantations.[26]

Whately wrote John Temple on August 14, asking questions about the planned "stamp duty, which unless unforeseen objections occur will probably be extended next year to America."

> It will be a principal object of attention here to make this tax as little burthensome as possible, but for this purpose it will be necessary to know whether the same duties as are imposed in England . . . would be too heavy on the Colonies.

Temple responded on September 10. His response is of particular significance since he was an important British official in America: surveyor general of customs for the five northern colonies.

> Consider Great Brittain & her Colonies on the larger scale, & see whither it will be expedient or prudent to lay such a duty. It is a certain fact that the produce of all these Colonies in the course of trade goes now to Great Brittain for her manufactories, and if they produced three times as much as they do it would all go for the same purpose.

He points out that tax revenue would reduce American purchases as a pound-for-pound monetary loss:

> Our people are extravagantly fond of shew & dress, and have no bounds to their importation of Brittish manufactories but their want of money. Suppose a stamp tax to take place & to yield sixty thousand a year to be collected in America & sent home, here would certainly be £60,000 worth of goods less imported from Great Brittain.[27]

On December 6, Whately presented a draft plan to the lords commissioners of the Treasury, "Mr. Whately's Plan of a Stamp Act for the Colonies & Plantations in America and the West Indies."[28] It stated that

> A stamp act in the Colonies differs from those in England only in the rates with which the several subjects of this duty are to be charged. . . . The powers of officers and the penalties that experience has shown to be necessary for the prevention of frauds and evasions must be nearly the same there as in England. A bill comprehending all these clauses is already drawn and nothing therefore remains unsettled but the rates and the mode of distribution.[29]

The plan was approved before the end of the month.

Governing the Colonies

In the summer of 1764, Governor Bernard and Lieutenant Governor Hutchinson separately set down their ideas on matters of governance and the proper role of the colonies. These writings reveal the mindset of the two Massachusetts officials and help explain their decisions and actions.

On June 23, Bernard wrote to Secretary at War Lord Barrington, enclosing a treatise he had written regarding the colonies. Barrington was a combination of patron, friend, and sounding board to Bernard. He was a highly regarded ministerial officer of wide experience who was no friend of the colonies.

> Ever since I have been in America I have studied the Policy of the sevral Governments & endeavourd to acquire a true Idea of their Relation to Great Britain. . . . This Spring I formed my thoughts into a kind of regular System, as concise and as argumentative as could well be.[30]

The treatise, *Principles of Law and Polity, Applied to the Government of the British Colonies in America*, consists of ninety-seven propositions related to "a Connection between the Seat of Empire and its Dependencies."

> 1. The Kingdom of Great Britain is imperial; that is, sovereign, and not subordinate to or dependent upon any earthly power.

The following two propositions state a truth held almost unanimously by British leaders, one that had been discussed and authoritatively stated by influential jurists in Great Britain:

> 2. In all imperial states there resides somewhere or other an absolute power, which we will call the Sovereignty.
> 3. The Sovereignty of Great Britain is in the King in Parliament; that is, in the King acting with the advice and consent of the Lords and the Commons.

This clumsy phrase "King in Parliament" blurs the fact that since the latter part of the seventeenth century, sovereignty, including control over colonial policy, had been shifting from king to Parliament (the idea of a monarch refusing assent to something desired by Parliament was an obsolete aspect of the British constitution). Bernard makes a distinction between the rights of Englishmen in Great Britain from those who chose to settle in new territories.

> 29. The rule that a British subject shall not be bound by laws, or liable to taxes, but what he has consented to by his representatives, must be confined to the inhabitants of Great Britain only; and is not strictly true even there.
> 30. The Parliament of Great Britain, as well from its rights of

> Sovereignty as from occasional exigencies, has a right to make laws for, and impose taxes upon, its subjects in its external dominions, although they are not represented in such Parliament.

His idea of imposition of internal taxes is at odds with later parliamentary policy.

> 44. Although the right of the Parliament of Great Britain, to raise taxes in any parts of the British Empire, is not to be disputed; yet it would be most advisable to leave to the Provincial Legislatures the raising the internal taxes.

This next assertion is dramatic, denying the repeated statements in charters promising settlers the rights held by British subjects in the realm.

> 60. There are some rights and privileges which the British subjects, in the external dominions, *are not equally capable of enjoying* with those residing in Great Britain.

He ends with the need for greater British governmental authority in the colonies.

> 97. This is therefore the proper and critical time to reform the American governments upon a general, constitutional, firm, and durable plan; and if it is not done now, it will probably every day grow more difficult, till at last it becomes impracticable.[31]

Barrington responded on October 3: "I have presented your work to Lord Halifax who admires it greatly, and says it is the best thing of the kind by much that he ever read."[32] Bernard also sent a copy (which he called "Summary of American Policy") to Richard Jackson on July 9. Although he was "particularly desirous not to be publickly known as the Writer of this Paper," he suggested some private circulation and even hinted that it might deserve wider publication.[33]

Lieutenant Governor Hutchinson wrote an essay in mid-July expressing his ideas about the relationship between the mother country and the colonies. The essay, written in the form of a letter from a concerned gentleman to an imagined friend, is now known as *A Brief State of the Claim of the Colonies and the Interest of the Nation with Respect to Them.*[34] Hutchinson sent it to Richard Jackson in early September, making it clear that he was to use the essay as he saw fit in terms of its arguments but was not to reveal the author.[35]

The letter begins with a discussion about the rights of colonists compared to "fellow Subjects in the mother Country."

> British Colonies should ever remain subject to the controul of Britain & consequently must be bound by the determinations of the supreme authority there: the British parliament. . . . [It] is possible for such a parliament to pass Acts which may abridge British Subjects of what are generally called natural rights.

This seems drastic, but "such is the [wisdom] & justice of a British Parliament that in all Acts a tender [regard will] be had to all rights natural & acquired of every Subject."

> Colonists would not leave their native Country until it was stipulated & agreed [by charter] . . . that they should have Assemblies of their own chusing to [make] laws for their government, to raise monies by taxes, &c . . . [and] should enjoy all the privileges & immunities of free & natural Subjects.

In consequence of such agreements, the colonists "claim a power of making Law & a privilege of exemption from taxes except by their own Representatives."

> This power & privilege they say is granted in express Terms in the Commissions & Charters & it is implied [to be the same as] privileges of natural born English Subjects.

However, he goes on that it "does not seem to be an unreasonable proposition, that the inhabitants of [a] Colony are intitled to all the privileges they enjoyed in their mother Country which will *consist with their dependance* upon it." He recognizes that "when the Parliament touches your interior parts by excises, Stamp Duties, poll taxes [and so on] you will have some reason to complain."

> I cannot help wondering at this distinction which I have often heard made by men every way superior to myself. Is it for the sake of regulating trade or to raise money from the Colonies that the Duties are laid by the late Act of Parliament [Sugar Act]?

He makes an argument that the intent must "be for the sake of the money arising from the Duties & if so how are the privileges of the people less affected than by an internal tax." He makes the point that there is *no significant difference between duties and internal taxes.*

> How are the Privileges of the People less affected [by the payment of duties] than by an internal tax? Is it any difference to me whether I pay three pounds ten shillings duty for a pipe of wine to an officer of Impost or whether I pay the same Sum by an excise of ninepence per Gall to an excise Officer?

He addresses the issue of representation in the colonies. Although only a small number of subjects in Britain can vote, he argues that every interest in Britain "is represented & the concern of particular Members or set of Members in Parliament."

> [But] what Member can be said to be the representative of the Colonies more than all the rest? Are not the Colonies considered as detached & having a distinct interest from the Interest of the Nation?

Although he recognizes the lack of representation in the colonies, he is not necessarily sympathetic—colonial rights are not absolute.

> Whatever opinion we [Americans] have of our Rights the parliament must be the final Judges & it is possible that it may be determined that the *natural right of a Colonist is not the same with the natural right of an Inhabitant of Britain* & that the Colonists have no sufficient Plea from their charters . . . for exemption from parliamentary taxes.

His assertion regarding the natural right of a colonist is anathema to Americans. This is equivalent to Bernard's proposition #60 that American rights are not equal "with those residing in Great Britain."

Two

Protest

"The resolution of the House of Commons . . . asserting their rights to establish stamp duties, and internal taxes, to be collected in the colonies without their own consent, hath much more, and for much more reason, alarmed the British subjects in America than anything that had ever been done before."

—Rhode Island governor Stephen Hopkins, November 1764

IN LATE 1764, Americans protested that the planned stamp duties were beyond the authority of Parliament: a violation of *the rights of Englishmen.* The constitutional argument comes down to this: It is "the undoubted Right of Englishmen, that no Taxes be imposed on them, but with their own Consent, given personally, or by their Representatives." Nine colonies made some form of protest in 1764 to the Grenville program, five being petitions to Parliament or the king. The colonies protested against both the Sugar Act (the economic burden) and planned stamp duties (a violation of their rights). There are repeated themes, even phrases, the repetition being important to the story in order to emphasize that there was a growing American consensus regarding parliamentary taxation.

Overture

In August 1764, Richard Bland, one of the leading citizens of Virginia and an influential member of the House of Burgesses, published a pamphlet: *The Colonel Dismounted . . . Containing a Dissertation upon the Constitution of the Colony.*[1] In an attempt to define the exclusive powers of colonial government, Bland deals with a central constitutional issue: the division of authority between Parliament and the colonial legislatures. He does so by making a distinction between internal and external spheres of government.

Bland first makes the point that Virginians "are the descendants of Englishmen" who settled "this new region for the benefit and aggrandizement of the parent kingdom." The rights of English subjects "must be derived to us from them," and that such rights "could not be forfeited by their migration to America." All colonial protests made the same point that subjects in the colonies had the same rights as their fellow subjects who remained in Great Britain.

> Under an English government all men are born free, are only subject to laws made with their own consent, and cannot be deprived of the benefit of these laws without a transgression of them. . . . The people of this colony are freeborn and . . . must necessarily have a legal constitution, that is, a legislature, composed in part, of the representatives of the people who may enact laws for the INTERNAL government of the colony.

Bland defines internal government in terms of the power or authority of the legislature of the colony. He first establishes what the legislature cannot do.

> By the term INTERNAL government it may be easily perceived that I exclude from the legislature of the colony all power derogatory to their dependence upon the mother kingdom; for as we cannot lose the rights of Englishmen by our removal to this continent, so neither can we withdraw our dependence without destroying the constitution.

On that basis, he admits the broad authority of Parliament to make law in the external sphere of government—but he simultaneously imposes a limitation.

> In every instance, therefore, of our EXTERNAL government we are and must be subject to the authority of the British Parliament, but in no others; for if the Parliament should impose laws upon us merely relative to our INTERNAL government, it deprives us, as far as those laws extend, of the most valuable part of our birthright as Englishmen, of being governed by laws made with our own consent.

He continues to build on the internal/external model to further establish a boundary to the rightful authority of Parliament.

> As all power, therefore, is excluded from the colony of withdrawing its dependence from the mother kingdom, so is all power over the colony excluded from the mother kingdom but such as respects its EXTERNAL government. I do not deny but that the Parliament, as the stronger power, can force any Laws it shall think fit upon us; but the inquiry is not what it can do, but what constitutional right it has to do so: And if it has not any constitutional right, then any *tax respecting our INTERNAL polity which may hereafter be imposed on us by act of Parliament, is arbitrary, as depriving us of our rights, and may be opposed.*

After all that, he makes this expansive declaration of the authority of a colonial legislature.

> From these principles, which I take to be incontrovertible, as they are deduced from the nature of the English constitution, it is evident that the legislature of the colony have a right to enact ANY law they shall think necessary for their INTERNAL government.[2]

Although Bland did not define exactly what he meant by internal and external government, it is clear "that Parliament's authority—to legislate as well as to tax—stopped short of the Atlantic coast of the colonies and did not extend over any affair relating exclusively to the internal life of the colonies."[3]

NEW YORK

On September 4, 1764, New York lieutenant governor Cadwallader Colden opened the fall session of the General Assembly with a mundane recitation of minor governmental tasks. The assembly responded to Colden on September 11. Their address started with some mild comments and compliments to the king, "our most gracious Sovereign," but then an expression of confidence in his protecting their rights transformed into a tirade against taxation. They hoped to be saved from "the deplorable state of that wretched people, who (being taxed by a power subordinate to none, and in a great degree unacquainted with their circumstances) can call nothing their own." They spoke directly to the lieutenant governor.

> We hope your Honor will join with us in an endeavour to secure that great Badge of English Liberty of being taxed only with our Consent; to which, we conceive, all His Majesty's Subjects at home and abroad equally entitled.[4]

On September 20, Colden wrote to the Board of Trade.

> This Address of the Assembly appeared to me so undutiful and indecent that I think it incumbent on me to give your Lordships a particular account of my Conduct thereon. As soon as I discovered the tenor of the Address I endeavoured . . . to dissuade them from inserting suggestions which I think highly disrespectful to the Legislature of Great Britain.[5]

The General Assembly of New York was the first to prepare petitions to king and Parliament, approved on October 18. The petition to the House of Commons was the most important, a bold protest later considered to be "conceived in terms so inflammatory" that no member of the House of Commons was willing to introduce it. It not only denied the authority of Parliament to levy internal taxes but also denied authority to levy customs duties for the purpose of revenue—the only colony to explicitly do so in 1764.

The petition starts by saying that they have received news that Parliament may "impose Taxes upon the Subjects here, by Laws to be passed there." New York denies Parliament that right, demanding "an Exemption from the Burthen of all Taxes not granted by themselves."

> An Exemption from the Burthen of ungranted, involuntary Taxes must be the grand Principle of every free State. Without such a Right vested in themselves, exclusive of all others, there can be no Liberty, no Happiness, no Security; it is inseparable from the very Idea of Property, for who can call that his own which may be taken away at the Pleasure of another?
>
> May we proceed to inform the Commons of Great Britain . . . that the People of this Colony . . . nobly disdain the thought of claiming that Exemption as a Privilege. They found it on a Basis more honourable, solid and stable; they challenge it, and glory in it as their Right.

Since a Parliament *there* is taxing a people *here*, the burden will be unjust, even tyrannical.

> No History can furnish an Instance of a Constitution to permit one Part of a Dominion to be taxed by another, and that too in Effect, but by a Branch of that other Part, who in all Bills for public Aids, suffer not the least Alteration. And if such an absurd and unequal Constitution should be adopted, who . . . cannot foresee, that while the People on one Side of the Atlantic enjoy an Exemption from the Load, those on the other must submit to the most unsupportable Oppression and Tyranny.

Next is a transition to issues of trade and duties, beginning with acceptance of the rationale behind the British-mandated laws of trade, the Navigation Act.

> The Authority of the Parliament of Great Britain to model the Trade of the whole Empire so as to subserve the Interest of her own we are ready to recognize in the most extensive and positive Terms. [For example] the Colonies cannot, would not, ask for a Licence to import woolen Manufactures from France.

But trade not in conflict with trade of Great Britain is a different matter.

> A Freedom to drive all Kinds of Traffick in a Subordination to, and not inconsistent with, the British Trade; and an Exemption from all Duties in such a Course of Commerce, is humbly claimed by the Colonies, as the most essential of all the Rights to which they are intitled, as Colonists from, and connected, in the common Bond of Liberty, with the unenslaved Sons of Great Britain.

The petition restates and emphasizes that Parliament can regulate trade but can neither tax nor levy duties for the purpose of revenue.

> Since all Impositions, whether they be internal Taxes or Duties paid for what we consume, equally diminish the Estates upon which they are charged; what avails it to any People, by which of them they are impoverished? Every Thing will be given up to preserve Life; and though there is a Diversity in the Means, yet, the *whole Wealth of a Country may be as effectually drawn off by the Exaction of Duties, as by any other Tax upon their Estates.*

This statement shows that the General Assembly has considerable insight into the related issues of taxation and the levy of duties by Parliament. New York goes on to state that duties limited to the regulation of trade are not objectionable.

> Parliament [should] charge our Commerce with no other Duties than a necessary Regard to the particular Trade of Great-Britain evidently demands; but leave it to the legislative Power of the Colony to impose all other Burthens upon it's own People, which the publick Exigences may require.

Any customs duty that is not of benefit to the trade of Great Britain—one that is levied for the purpose of revenue—is an abuse of authority: it is unconstitutional taxation. This line of thinking ends with a bit of wry understatement: "Latterly, the Laws of Trade seem to have been framed without an Attention to this fundamental Claim."[6]

Connecticut

In May 1764, the Connecticut General Assembly appointed a committee led by Governor Thomas Fitch "to collect and set in the most advantageous light all such arguments and objections as may justly and reasonably [be] advanced against creating and collecting a revenue in America, more particularly in this Colony, and especially against effecting the same by Stamp Duties." The result was an essay published as a pamphlet approved by the assembly in late October: *Reasons why the British Colonies in America should not be charged with Internal Taxes.*[7] (Fitch was the primary author, later turning it into the Connecticut petition to the House of Commons.) The essay deals with *internal* taxation only, Fitch never even using the phrase *external* taxation (but even without using the phrase he is distinguishing one from the other).

The argument against internal taxation is based on the usual need for consent: "By the Common Law of England, every Commoner hath a Right not to be subjected to Laws made without his Consent." But consent "cannot be given by every individual Man in Person, therefore is the Power of rendering such Consent lodged in the Hands of Representatives, by them elected and chosen for that Purpose."

> It is a clear Point that the Colonies may not, they cannot, be represented in Parliament; and . . . that "NO LAWS CAN BE MADE OR ABROGATED, WITHOUT THE CONSENT OF THE PEOPLE, BY THEIR REPRESENTATIVES."

Along the way, Fitch makes the point of the pamphlet: "That charging Stamp Duties or other internal Taxes on the Colonies in America by parliamentary Authority will be an Infringement of . . . Rights and Privileges, and deprive the Colonists of their Freedom and Inheritance." But more important for understanding his position is his rationale.

> If these internal Taxations take Place, and the Principles upon which they must be founded are adopted and carried into Execution the Colonies will have no more than a Shew of Legislation left, nor the King's Subjects in them any more than the Shadow of true English Liberty; for the same Principles which will justify such a Tax of a Penny, will warrant a Tax of a Pound, an hundred, or a thousand Pounds, and so on without Limitation; and if they will warrant a Tax on one Article, they will support one on as many Particulars as shall be thought necessary to raise any Sum proposed.

He sees a potential objection.

> Perhaps it may be here objected that these Principles, if allowed, *will prove too much* [and hence deny that Parliament] has a Superintendency over all the Colonies and Plantations abroad, and Right to govern and controul them as shall be thought best.

But it turns out that the "clear Point" introduced above that "no laws can be made" applies only to what Bland referred to as internal government. Fitch contends that the actions of Parliament in the external sphere do not require the consent of the colonists.

> Parliament by its *supreme and general Jurisdiction*, may justly order and do some Things, which may affect the Property of the American Subjects, in a Way which, in some Sense, may be said to be independent upon or without the Will or Consent of the People, as by *Regulations of Trade and Commerce* and the like; and by general Orders relative to and Restrictions of their Conduct for the Good of the Whole.

Since "the Colonies are so many Governments independent of each other . . . they can only establish Regulations within and for themselves respectively." Further,

> as they are all subordinate to and dependent upon the Mother Country, Propriety, Conveniency and even Necessity require that they should be subject to some *General Superintendency and Controul* in order that the general Course of their Trade and Business should be so uniform as to center in some general national Interest.

Therefore, "it becomes plainly expedient that there should be some supreme Director over all His Majesty's Dominions; and this Character and Authority, all Men must acknowledge and allow, properly belong to the British Parliament." Fitch then transforms the authority for "Regulations of Trade and Commerce" into unfettered levy of duties—no consent required.

> It is humbly conceived that the Subjects in the Colonies may enjoy their Rights, Privileges and Properties, as Englishmen, and yet, for political Reasons, be restrained from some particular Correspondence or Branches of Trade and Commerce, or may be subjected therein to such Duties, Charges and Regulations *as the supreme Power may judge proper* to establish as so many Conditions of enjoying such Trade. Reasons of State may render it expedient to prohibit some Branches of Trade and to burden others.

Fitch provides further rationale that "if Restrictions on Navigation, Commerce, or other external Regulations only are established, the *internal Government* . . . will be and continue in the Substance of them whole and entire." Fitch ends with the hope that Parliament will "have a tender regard for the rights and immunities of the King's subjects in the American colonies and charge no internal taxations upon them without their consent."[8]

Massachusetts' Lieutenant Governor Hutchinson disagreed with the position taken by Connecticut regarding internal and external taxation (consistent with his essay *A Brief State of the Claim of the Colonies*): external taxes violate the rights of the colonists, just as do internal taxes. On November 9, he wrote to his friend Ebenezer Silliman, a collaborator with Fitch on the preparation of the essay. He points out that "the professed design of the duties by the late Act [i.e., the Sugar Act] is to raise a revenue." He sees no benefit, indeed danger (a problem Fitch has ignored but New York identified), to the protest against internal taxes while conceding to Parliament the right to raise revenue by the imposition of "duties on trade enough to drain us so thoroughly that it will not be possible to pay internal taxes as a revenue to them or even to support government within ourselves."[9]

Massachusetts

At a Boston town meeting on May 24, 1764, a committee led by patriot firebrand Samuel Adams prepared instructions to the Boston delegates in the Massachusetts legislature.

> We cannot help expressing our surprize, that when so early notice was given by the Agent of the intention of the Ministry to burthen us with new Taxes, so little regard was had to this most interesting Matter, that the Court was not even called together to consult about it till the latter end of the Year, the consequence of which was, that Instructions could not be sent to the Agent, though solisited by him, till the Evil had got beyond an easy remedie.

The danger is new taxation.

> But what still hightens our Apprehensions is that those unexpected proceedings may be preparitory to new Taxations upon us; For if our Trade may be taxed why not our Lands? Why not the produce of our Lands and every Thing we possess or make use of? This we apprehend annihilates our Charter Right to Govern and Tax ourselves. It strikes at our British Privileges which as we have never forfeited them we hold in common with our Fellow Subjects who are Natives of Britain. If Taxes are laid upon us in any shape without ever having a Legal Representation where they are laid, are we not reduced from the Character of Free Subjects to the miserable state of tributary Slaves?

A specific instruction:

> As his Majestys other Northern American Colonys are embark'd with us in this most important Bottom, we further desire you to use your Endeavors, that their weight may be added To that of this Province; that by the united Applications of all who are Aggrieved, All may happily obtain Redress.[10]

The House of Representatives (the assembly) convened on May 30: "Mr. Speaker communicated sundry Letters from Mr. Agent Mauduit."

> Ordered, That [a committee, including Otis, Thacher, Cushing] take the Letters and Papers under Consideration, together with the Letters receiv'd last Year, and make Report.

On June 13, the committee submitted its work as a letter to Mauduit.

> The House of Representatives have received your several Letters of the *30th of December,* the 11th of February, the *13th*

> *of March* and the 23d of March last. The Contents are to the last degree alarming. In that of the 30th of December, you seem to wonder at the silence of the House.
>
> No Agent of this Province has Power to make express Concessions in any case without express Orders. And the Silence of the Province should have been imputed to any Cause, even to Despair, rather than be construed into a tacit Cession of their Rights, or an Acknowledgment of a Right in the Parliament of Great-Britain to impose Duties and Taxes upon a People who are not represented in the Houfe of Commons.

More lecturing:

> If all the Colonists are to be Taxed at Pleasure, without any Representative in Parliament, what will there be to distinguish them in point of Liberty from the Subjects of the most absolute Prince? If we are to be Taxed at Pleasure without our Consent, will it be any Consolation to us, that we are to be assessed by an Hundred instead of One? If we are not Represented, we are Slaves.

They address Mauduit's letter of March 13 and the postponement of the stamp duties.

> The actual laying the Stamp Duty, you say, is deferred 'till next Year, Mr. Greenville being willing to give the Provinces their Option to raise that, or some other equivalent Tax, desirous, as he was pleased to express himself, "to consult the Ease, the Quiet, and the Good-will of the Colonies."
>
> If the Ease, the Quiet and Good-will of the Colonies are of any Importance to Great-Britain, no Measures could be hit upon that have a more natural and direct Tendency to enervate those Principles than the Resolutions you inclose. The kind Offer of suspending this Stamp Duty in the Manner, and upon the Condition you mention, amounts to no more than this, that if the Colonies will not Tax themselves as they may be directed, the Parliament will Tax them.

The committee includes direct instructions.

> You are to remonstrate against [the actions of Parliament], and if possible, to obtain a Repeal of the Sugar-Act, and prevent the Imposition of any further Duties or Taxes on these Colonies.

The letter ends:

> In a Word, a People may be free and tolerably happy without a particular Branch of Trade, but without the Priviledge of assessing their own Taxes, they can be neither.
> Inclosed, you will have a brief *State of the Rights of the Colonies*, drawn up by one of our Members, which you are to make the best use of in your Power, with the addition of such Arguments as your own good Sense will suggest.[11]

The *State of the Rights of the Colonies* was written by James Otis, the leader of the patriot, or radical, faction. It presents an argument based on natural rights: laws of nature and God as established in the British constitution.[12] "The absolute rights of Englishmen, as frequently declared in Parliament, from Magna Charta to this time, are the rights of personal security, personal liberty and of private property." By establishing the colonies in America, the colonists and their descendants, "By the laws of nature and of nations, the voice of universal reason, and of God," are entitled to those same rights.

> The colonists have been by their several charters declared natural subjects, and entrusted with the power of making their own local laws, not repugnant to the laws of England, and with the power of taxing themselves.

Otis argues "that the power of the British Parliament is held as sacred and as uncontrollable in the colonies as in England." But there are limits on that power.

> The question is not upon the general power or right of the Parliament, but whether it is not circumscribed within some equitable and reasonable bounds . . . which if exceeded their acts become those of mere power without right, and consequently void.[13]

Otis wrote a longer pamphlet in the summer of 1764: *The Rights of the British Colonies Asserted and Proved*, one of the most widely read and discussed pamphlets of this period. It is, however, often complex, confusing, and contradictory, even later refuted by Otis himself.[14]

On June 25, the assembly wrote the other colonies, being "desirous of the united Assistance of the several Colonies in a Petition" opposed to British actions. Further, "that the Agents of the several Colonies might be directed . . . to unite in the most serious Remonstrance" against the Sugar Act and the proposed Stamp Act.[15]

On June 29, Governor Bernard reported to the Board of Trade detailing the recent votes of the assembly: "The House of Representatives proceeded to give separate instructions to the Agent [i.e., the letter of June 13], without so much as asking the Council to join with them." Regarding the June 25 letter to other colonies, he sees that it is intended

> to lay a foundation for connecting the demagogues of the several Governments in America to join together in opposition to all orders from Great Britain which don't square with their notions of the rights of the people. Perhaps I may be too suspicious; a little time will show whether I am or not.[16]

Time showed he was not too suspicious. The invitation had no immediate effect, but it did lay a foundation. In only "a little time" (one year) a similar letter will prompt a gathering of "the demagogues" in an important meeting: a congress of the colonies.

By October, the assembly had prepared a protest to the king and both houses of Parliament, primarily protesting the recent duties of the Sugar Act. The duties and regulations of the Sugar Act will "destroy our trade, & as we humbly conceive deprive us of the most essential rights of Britons." The protest included the assertion, "that *we look upon those duties as a tax*, and which we humbly apprehend ought not to be laid without the representatives of the people affected by them."

> Now we have ever supposed this to be one essential right of British subjects, that they shall not be subjected to taxes which, in person or by representative, they have no voice in laying.
>
> In this conclusion we have been fortified by the practise of the English Parliaments in former and later times, which have ever vindicated this right, and have never laid any duty or tax on the subjects of Ireland, though that hath ever been deemed & acknowlegeth itself to be a dependent Kingdom.[17]

That draft address, sent to the council for concurrence on October 22, was rejected; the council thought that the denial of parliamentary authority over taxation, and particularly the identification of duties as being taxes, would do more harm than good. The petition resulting from conference—the formal position of Massachusetts—was developed under the influence of Lieutenant Governor Hutchinson who insisted that the petition avoid any hint of opposition to the use of duties for the purpose of raising revenue; and no mention of "rights" held by the colonists.

The resulting compromise petition was approved on November 3 and addressed to the House of Commons only. There was no complaint about the unconstitutional nature of the levy of taxes, only that the duties planned for the Sugar Act would have the effect of an absolute prohibition. When the subject of internal taxes was slowly raised, the address showed gratitude for the tenderness "of the legislature of Great Britain of the liberties of the subjects in the colonies." The plea for relief was meek. They "humbly hope the colonies in general have so demeaned themselves . . . still to deserve the continuance of all those liberties which they have hitherto enjoyed." And they hoped "that the *privileges* of the colonies relative to their internal taxes which they have so long enjoyed may still be continued to them."[18] In the end, Massachusetts made no constitutional objection to the duties of the Sugar Act or to the planned internal taxation of the Stamp Act.

That Hutchinson was the strongest force behind the wording of the petition, and that it is at odds with Hutchinson's letter to Sillman of November 9, indicates the degree to which the Massachusetts posture to Parliament was political in nature, hoping that a polite request might relieve them from the burden of stamp duties.

Thomas Cushing (a patriot leader and influential member of the assembly) wrote Mauduit on November 17 to downplay the importance of the petition.

> The House of Representatives were clearly for making an ample and full declaration of the exclusive Right of the People of the Colonies to tax themselves and that they ought not to be deprived of a right they had so long enjoyed and which they held by Birth and by Charter; but they could not prevail with the Councill, tho they made several Tryalls, to be more explicit than they have been in the Petition sent you.

Cushing gives Mauduit this instruction.

> Considering they had wrote you fully upon the matter of Right the last session [on June 13] and had sent you a small tract entitled, *The Rights of the British Colonies* in general . . . which they then desired and expected you would make the best use of in your Power, they thought it the less necessary to remonstrate by themselves at this time. . . . You will therefore collect the sentiments of the Representative Body of People rather from what they have heretofore sent you than from the present Address.[19]

This is a stunning statement, recanting support of the November petition in favor of their earlier stance sent to Mauduit in the letter of June 13. Although that letter was not the official position of Massachusetts, British leaders became aware of it and saw it as an important statement, perhaps giving a more accurate representation of the position of the colony than the bland official petition.

In a letter to Pownall on May 6, 1765, Bernard—comparing the November petition to the letter of June 13—admitted that "I was in hopes that the Petition . . . would have made amends for the letter of the house only to the Agent: but I find that the latter had made too deep impressions to be easily obliterated."[20]

Hutchinson's opinion of the New York petition provides further insight into his thinking about the humble and gentle manner in which Massachusetts voiced its complaint. The following is a letter to Richard Jackson in the Hutchinson letter book (entered late November) but marked "not sent." He presumably had second thoughts about committing such blunt words to a letter, but they nonetheless reflect his state of mind.

> Since I sent you copy of the petition from this province one of the Representatives of N York has been in town & brot with him copy of the address from the Representatives there. It is said by some Zealots here to be a very spirited performance but really it is the most extraordinary thing I ever saw & not only discovers the authors of it to be unacquainted with all form of proceeding in such cases but that they are strangers to the rules of decency & good manners.[21]

RHODE ISLAND

On November 29, the Rhode Island assembly adopted a petition to the king. The colonies were alarmed about the

> resolution to establish stamp duties and other internal taxes to be collected within them. This design carried into execution, we humbly conceive, would tend to deprive us of our just and long enjoyed rights. We have hitherto possessed . . . equal freedom with Your Majesty's subjects in Britain; whose essential privilege it is to be governed only by laws to which themselves have some way consented.

This summary of the petition makes three key points based on equitable treatment.

> That our trade may be restored to its former condition, and no further limited, restrained and burdened, than becomes necessary for the general good of all Your Majesty's subjects;
>
> That the courts of vice admiralty may not be vested with more extensive powers in the colonies than are given them by law in Great Britain;
>
> That the colonists may not be taxed but by the consent of their own representatives, as Your Majesty's other free subjects are.[22]

In parallel with the petition to the king, Governor Stephen Hopkins wrote a related essay: *The Rights of Colonies Examined*.[23] It was approved by the General Assembly on November 30, first printed in the *Records of the Colony of Rhode Island*, and published in the *Providence Gazette* of December 22. It was reprinted by other colonial newspapers and issued as a pamphlet, including in a London edition.

Hopkins's principal assertion was that Americans could not be taxed by Parliament. In accordance with the British constitution, "British subjects are to be governed only agreeable to laws to which themselves have some way consented."

> On the contrary, those who are governed at the will of another, or of others, and whose property may be taken from them by taxes or otherwise without their own consent and against their will, are in the miserable condition of slaves.

He moves away from the specific idea of taxation to distinguish the roles of Parliament and the colonial legislatures. His thinking evokes that of Richard Bland in his distinction between internal and external spheres of government. Hopkins specifies the mandate of the colonial legislature as internal government: "In the first place, let it be considered that . . . each of the colonies hath a legislature within itself to take care of its interests and provide for its peace and internal government." He then limits the scope of internal government by defining external government.

> There are many *things of a more general nature*, quite out of the reach of these particular legislatures, which it is necessary should be regulated, ordered, and governed.
>
> One of this kind is the commerce of the whole British empire, taken collectively, and that of each kingdom and colony in it as it makes a part of that whole. Indeed, everything that concerns the proper interest and fit government of the whole commonwealth, of keeping the peace, and subordination of all the parts towards the whole and one among another, must be considered in this light.

He does not use the phrase *external government*, but "commerce of the whole British empire," and similar phrases certainly serve the same purpose.

> These, with *all other matters of a general nature*, it is absolutely necessary should have a general power to direct them; some supreme and over ruling authority, with power to make laws and form regulations for the good of all, and to compel their execution and observation.
>
> Certainly, such power includes regulation of trade [the Navigation Act] and use of customs duties to accomplish such regulation.
>
> It being necessary some such general power should exist somewhere, every man of the least knowledge of the British constitution will be naturally led to look for and find it in the Parliament of Great Britain. That grand and august legislative body must from the nature of their authority and the necessity of the thing be justly vested with this power.

He is using the word "power" in the sense of rightful authority.

> Hence it becomes the indispensable duty of every good and loyal subject cheerfully to obey and patiently submit to all the acts, laws, orders, and regulations that may be made and passed by Parliament for directing and governing all these general matters.

He does mean *only* general matters, thereby limiting the authority of Parliament. He returns to the immediate issue of 1764, stamp duties, essentially categorizing them as internal taxes.

> The resolution of the House of Commons, come into during the same session of Parliament, asserting their rights to establish stamp duties and internal taxes to be collected in the colonies without their own consent, hath much more, and for much more reason, alarmed the British subjects in America than anything that had ever been done before. These resolutions, carried into execution, the colonies cannot help but consider as a manifest violation of their just and long enjoyed rights. For it must be confessed by all men that they who are taxed at pleasure by others cannot possibly have any property, can have nothing to be called their own. They who have no property can have no freedom, but are indeed reduced to the most abject slavery.

He later refers to taxation by Parliament as being "invidious and unconstitutional." Close to the end he raises the issue of the power to levy duties for revenue.

> The Parliament, it is confessed, have power to regulate the trade of the whole empire; and hath it not full power, by this means, to draw all the money and all the wealth of the colonies into the mother country *at pleasure*?

Hopkins answers his question as yes, that they do have such full power. In fact, he uses that power to support his general argument; he makes the point that Parliament—having such ability to collect revenue from the colonies with duties—need not and ought not impose internal taxation.[24] He recognizes the importance of such power but makes no constitutional objection to duties imposed for the purpose of revenue.

VIRGINIA

The House of Burgesses met on October 30. Speaker John Robinson introduced the Massachusetts letter of June 25 (to which Virginia later responded in favorable terms). On November 14, the House of Burgesses approved resolves directing that an address to the king and memorials to Parliament be drawn up; the resolves themselves provide insight into the attitude of the Virginians.

First, the king.

> Resolved, That a most humble and dutiful Address be presented to his Majesty, imploring his Royal Protection of . . . their natural and civil Rights as men and as Descendants of Britons; *which Rights must be violated if Laws, respecting the internal government, and Taxation* of themselves, are imposed upon them by any other Power than that derived from their own Consent, by and with the Approbation of their Sovereign.

Second, the Lords.

> Resolved, That a Memorial be prepared to be laid before the Right Hon. the Lords Spiritual and Temporal in Parliament assembled, intreating their Lordships, by a proper and reasonable Interposition and Exertion of their Power, not to suffer the People of this Colony to be enslaved or oppressed by Laws respecting their *internal Polity*, and Taxes imposed on them in a Manner that is unconstitutional.

And third, the Commons.

> Resolved, That a Memorial be prepared to be laid before the Honourable the House of Commons, to assert, with decent

> Freedom, the Rights and Liberties of the People of this Colony as British Subjects, to remonstrate that Laws for their *internal Government, or Taxation, ought not to be imposed by any Power but what is delegated to their Representatives, chosen by themselves*. [Taxation by Parliament would be] a Violation of the most sacred and valuable Principle of the Constitution.[25]

The fundamental point is a request that Virginia be free from parliamentary taxation (all taxation, there being no distinction made between internal and external taxation).

The memorial to the king "intreats"

> that your Majesty will be graciously pleased to protect your People of this Colony in the Enjoyment of their *ancient and inestimable Right of being governed by such Laws respecting their internal Polity and Taxation as are derived from their own Consent.*

The right is long-standing and customary.

> [This is] a Right which as Men, and Descendants of Britons, they have ever quietly possessed since first by Royal Permission and Encouragement they left the Mother Kingdom to extend its Commerce and Dominion.

The memorial to the Lords:

> Your Memorialists conceive it to be a fundamental Principle of the British Constitution, without which Freedom can no Where exist, that the People are not subject to any Taxes but such as are laid on them by their own Consent, or by those who are legally appointed to represent them.

The rationale:

> Property must become too precarious for the Genius of a free People which can be taken from them at the Will of others,

> who cannot know what Taxes such People can bear, or the easiest Mode of raising them; and who are not under that Restraint, which is the greatest Security against a burthensome Taxation, when the Representatives themselves must be affected by every Tax imposed on the People.
>
> Your Memorialists have been invested with the Right of taxing their own People from the first Establishment of a regular Government in the Colony, and . . . they cannot now be deprived of a right they have so long enjoyed, and which they have never forfeited.

The remonstrance to the House of Commons starts with this observation. The House of Commons had resolved:

> that towards defending, protecting, and securing the British Colonies and Plantations in America, it may be proper to charge certain Stamp Duties in the said Colonies and Plantations.

And "that the same Subject, which was then declined, may be resumed and further pursued in a succeeding Session."
The Burgesses protest.

> They conceive it is essential to British Liberty that Laws imposing Taxes on the People ought not to be made without the Consent of Representatives chosen by themselves; who, at the same Time that they are acquainted with the Circumstances of their Constituents, sustain a Proportion of the Burthen laid on them.

They deny taxation by the distant legislature.

> The Remonstrants do not discern by what Distinction they can be deprived of that sacred Birthright and most valuable Inheritance by their Fellow Subjects, nor with what Propriety they can be taxed or affected in their Estates by the Parliament,

wherein they are not, and indeed cannot, constitutionally be represented.

The ending shows a mix of respect and firm conviction, balancing a soft phrase with a hard one: "From these Considerations, it is hoped that the Honourable House of Commons will not prosecute a Measure. . . ." After that *hope*, they boldly proclaim that "British Patriots will *never consent* to the Exercise of anti-constitutional Power."[26]

On December 24, Lieutenant Governor Francis Fauquier wrote the Board of Trade, referring to the resolutions and the address and memorials, that "the terms are very warm and indecent." Fauquier explains that "the Subject Matter of them is praying to be permitted to tax themselves. I thought it my Duty to give your Lordships the most early Intelligence of this Matter in my Power."[27]

Other Protests

Four colonies did not submit petitions to the king or Parliament, but demonstrated compatible beliefs, setting the stage for a consensus opinion of the colonies in 1765.

The South Carolina assembly on September 4 directed agent Charles Garth to oppose "laying a stamp duty, or any other tax by act of Parliament on the colonies." It offered this constitutional argument: "The first, and in our opinion the principal reason, against such a measure, is its inconsistency with that inherent right of every British subject, not to be taxed but by his own consent, or that of his representative."[28]

The New Jersey committee of correspondence wrote agent Joseph Sherwood on September 10 directing him to take the position that New Jersey looks "upon all Taxes laid upon us without our Consent as a fundamental infringement of the Rights and privileges Secured to us as English Subjects and by Charter."[29]

The Pennsylvania assembly sent agent Richard Jackson instructions on September 22. They wish to prevail "on the Parliament to lay aside their Intention of imposing Stamp Duties, or laying any other Impositions or Taxes whatsoever on the Colonies, which may be destructive of their respective Rights." To accomplish this, "exert your utmost Endeavours with the Ministry and Parliament to prevent any such Impositions and Taxes, or any other Impositions or Taxes on the Colonists from being laid by the Parliament, inasmuch as they neither are or can be represented, under their present Circumstances, in that Legislature."[30]

The North Carolina assembly, in a message to Governor Arthur Dobbs on October 31, complained of being "burthened with new Taxes and Impositions laid on us without our Privity and Consent, and against what we esteem our Inherent right and Exclusive privilege of Imposing our own Taxes."[31] The broad protest against "Impositions" can be read as an argument against duties for revenue (specifically the Sugar Act), joining the New York protest against customs duties for the purpose of revenue.

Three

Backlash

"The Acts and resolutions of the British Parliament were treated with indecent disrespect, and principles of a dangerous nature and tendency adopted and avowed."

—Board of Trade, December 1764

BRITISH LEADERS HEARD a sharp message in the American protests of late 1764: denial of the right of Parliament to tax the colonies; denial of "the very sovereignty of this kingdom." The British responded with outrage, the levy of stamp duties becoming less a matter of revenue than an assertion of parliamentary supremacy. An early warning is shown in a letter from Richard Waln, a merchant in London writing his brother in Philadelphia on September 12, 1764. The "late extraordinary proceedings of the Massachusetts government" were known to the ministry, "who with great warmth have expressed their displeasure. They esteem it a very high insult on government."[1]

American discontent, both about the Sugar Act and the prospect of future internal taxes, was widely known. On December 6 the *London Chronicle* reported news from the colonies.

> Boston (New England, Oct. 5)
> The late act of parliament (possibly for want of a thorough understanding) gives some uneasiness to the people of this province, and it is said of the northern colonies in general; and the fears of being taxed, internally, by the parliament, while we have no representation on the spot, are alarming to men of the greatest penetration and judgement among us.[2]

OFFICIAL PROCEEDINGS

On December 11, 1764, the Board of Trade reacted to events in America. Their journal presents the issue.

> Their lordships took into consideration the printed votes of the House of Representatives of the Province of Massachusets Bay in their last Session of Assembly, transmitted to the Board by Governor Bernard, as also a book therein referred to, and an address of the Assembly of New York to the Lieutenant Governor, and his answer thereto.

They conclude:

> It appearing to their lordships that in the said votes and address the Acts and resolutions of the British Parliament were treated with indecent disrespect, and principles of a dangerous nature and tendency adopted and avowed, it was agreed to lay the said papers before his Majesty in Council, and a representation to his Majesty thereupon was prepared, agreed to and signed.

The representation sent to the Privy Council the same day refers to "the printed Votes of the House of Representatives" of Massachusetts and specifically to the letter of June 13 to Mauduit "which, contrary to the usual practice was without the concurrence of the Governor and Council."

> In which letter the Acts and Resolutions of the Legislature of Great Britain are, we humbly conceive, treated with the most

> indecent disrespect, [and] principles of the most dangerous nature and tendency openly avowed.

In addition, the board forwards "a book referred to therein, printed & published at Boston and since reprinted and published in London."

> We likewise crave leave humbly to lay before your Majesty the Copy of an Address of the Assembly of New York to the Lieutenant Governor of that Province, and of his prudent and becoming answer thereto; in which address the said Assembly avow opinions and make declarations of the same dangerous tendency with those of the Assembly of the Massachusetts Bay.

The board reaches this overall judgment.

> These proceedings [are] calculated to raise groundless suspicion & distrust in the minds of your Majesty's good subjects in the Colonies, and have the strongest tendency to subvert those principles of constitutional relation & dependance upon which the Colonies were originally established.

But they make no recommendation for action, only advising "such measures as your Majesty shall in your great wisdom and with the advice of your Council think most prudent and necessary."[3]

On December 12, the Privy Council took into consideration the representation from the Board of Trade,

> together with several Votes *of the House of Representatives* of the Province of Massachusets Bay, of the 1st, 8th, 12th and 13th of June 1764, and also an Address of the General Assembly of the Colony of New York, to the Lieutenant Governor of that Colony, dated the 11th of September 1764.

They reached a conclusion on December 19.

> It is a matter of the *highest consequence to the Kingdom*, and the Legislature of Great Britain, and worthy the Consideration

> of Parliament; and to that end, that it may be adviseable for Your Majesty to give Directions that the same be laid before the Parliament.[4]

JUSTIFICATION FOR TAXATION

While British officials were expressing irritation and anger with the colonial protests, Thomas Whately was writing the most comprehensive justification for the authority of Parliament to tax the colonies. His arguments were put forth in a 114-page pamphlet: *The Regulations Lately Made concerning the Colonies*.[5] Intended as a refutation of colonial protests of 1764, it was an explanation and defense of actions taken by Parliament. It also presented the rationale for the tax planned to be levied in 1765. Initially published anonymously in January 1765, and at first thought to be written by Grenville himself, it was little short of an official statement of the government.

The bulk of the pamphlet deals with the Sugar Act, but in the final pages Whately notes that "upon no Calculation can [the Sugar Act revenue] be supposed to be equal to the Demand that must be made upon the Colonies; and therefore a further Tax has been proposed." Specifically, "It has been even resolved by a Vote of the House of Commons, that it may be proper to charge certain Stamp Duties in the Plantations; and here the Legislature stoped last Sessions out of Tenderness to the Colonies." It goes on to say that

> This Mode of Taxation is the easiest, the most equal and the most certain that can be chosen; The Duty falls chiefly upon Property; but it is spread lightly over a great Variety of Subjects, and lies heavy upon none: The Act executes itself by annulling the Instruments that have not paid the small Sums they are charged with; and the Tax thus supported and secured, is collected by few Officers, without Expence to the Crown, or Oppression on the People.

Whately makes detailed arguments to justify the need for American revenue, eventually reaching this point and setting the stage for refuting a standard argument against parliamentary taxation.

> The Reasonableness, and even the Necessity of requiring an American Revenue being admitted, the Right of the Mother Country to impose such a Duty upon her Colonies, if duly considered, cannot be questioned. [The colonies claim] the Privilege, which is common to all British Subjects, of being *taxed only with their own Consent, given by their Representatives.*

He elaborates on consequences of the "Privilege."

> No new Law whatever can bind us [British subjects] that is made without the Concurrence of our Representatives [here meaning Parliament]. The Acts of Trade and Navigation, and all other Acts that relate either to ourselves or to the Colonies, are founded upon no other Authority. *They are not obligatory if a Stamp Act is not,* and every Argument in support of an Exemption from the Superintendance of the British Parliament in the one Case, is equally applicable to the others.

Here is the idea of virtual representation, hence binding the colonies to the decisions of Parliament: "The Inhabitants of the Colonies are represented in Parliament: they do not indeed chuse the Members of that Assembly; neither are Nine Tenths of the People of Britain Electors."

> The Colonies are in exactly the same Situation. All British Subjects are really in the same; none are actually, all are virtually represented in Parliament; for every Member of Parliament sits in the House, not as Representative of his own Constituents, but as one of that august Assembly by which the Commons of Great Britain are represented. Their Rights and their Interests, however his own Borough may be affected by general Dispositions, ought to be the great Objects of his Attention, and the only Rules for his Conduct.[6]

This scheme of virtual representation, later used by Grenville in his proposal for stamp duties, was poorly thought out. Whately implicitly admits that taxes can be levied only on those represented, but it was easy to refute the idea of colonial representation. The claim that the colonies were virtually represented was an issue for only two years, calling forth essays and pamphlets both pro and con. It was American arguments that prevailed, decisively refuting the idea that the House of Commons represented the colonies. The concept was later abandoned by the British in favor of basing taxation on the need for a supreme legislature—including taxation authority—in any government.

Mitigate Backlash?

Realizing that Parliament was likely to reject any petition objecting to parliamentary taxation, the agents discussed how they might approach the ministry to lessen the blow to the colonies. South Carolina agent Charles Garth organized a coordinated effort, writing on December 26, 1764.

> I intend soon to propose a general meeting in order to consider of the proper steps to be taken in case the intended Stamp Bill should be brought into Parliament, for my opinion is as the Colonies oppose, they ought to oppose upon a point of this importance in such manner as most to command the attention of the Legislature.[7]

On January 16, 1765, Mauduit wrote to his clients about discussions with ministers, other agents, and merchants.

> All the servants of power say they don't desire to oppress, but seem determined that the colonies shall pay their Share of the National Expence; and I fear the Majority and Minority will both agree in this. *The Merchants talk much, but cannot bring them to act.* They say why don't the Agents write, apply, and take the Lead? The Agents say the Merchants will be much better attended to than they.[8]

The reluctance of the merchants to act is of particular significance because (as we shall see) in less than a year those merchants will become powerful allies in the movement to repeal the Stamp Act.

Garth, recently elected a member of the House of Commons, wrote South Carolina on February 8 about his efforts in January, "meeting and consulting with the agents as to the mode and measure of opposition to be given to the Stamp Bill, *all of us having instructions to support the rights and privileges of the Colonies and to dispute as it were the power of Parliament.*" Since "most of the Colonies had signify'd their inclinations to assist their Mother Country upon proper requisitions from hence . . . it was agreed it might have a good effect to have that inclination made known to Administration."[9]

The agents decided to call on Grenville, who set the meeting for February 2. Jared Ingersoll, who had arrived in London in early December 1764 and was now agent for Connecticut (in addition to Jackson), wrote Governor Fitch a lengthy letter on February 11, including describing the meeting.

> The Agents of the Colonies have had several Meetings, at one of which they were pleased to desire Mr. Franklin & myself as having lately Come from America & knowing more Intimately the Sentiments of the people, to wait on Mr. Grenville, together with Mr. Jackson & Mr. Garth who being Agents are also Members of Parliament, to remonstrate against the Stamp Bill, & to propose in Case any Tax must be laid upon America, that the several Colonies might be permitted to lay the Tax themselves.

Ingersoll put a positive twist on the meeting.

> Mr. Grenville gave us a full hearing—told us he took no pleasure in giving the Americans so much uneasiness as he found he did—that it was the Duty of his Office to manage the revenue—that he really was made to beleive that considering ye whole of the Circumstances of the Mother Country & the Colonies, the later could and ought to pay something, & that he knew of no better way than that now pursuing to lay such Tax, but that if we could tell of a better he would adopt it.

The agents advocated the use of requisitions from the king, then pointed out other problems with the bill, beyond the issue of taxation.

> Mr. Jackson told him plainly that he foresaw the Measure now pursuing [would enable] the Crown to keep up an armed Force of its own in America & to pay the Governours in the Kings Governments & all with the Americans own Money. [Therefore] the Assemblies in the Colonys would be subverted—that the Govrs. would have no Occasion, as for any Ends of their own or of the Crown, to call 'Em & that they never would be called together in the Kings Governments. Mr. Grenville warmly rejected the thought, said no such thing was intended nor would, he believed, take place.

Grenville returned to the suggestion that the colonies lay the tax themselves: "Mr. Grenville asked us if we could agree upon the several proportions Each Colony should raise. We told him no." (Of course, the answer was no; the question was pointless other than to emphasize that an attempted use of requisitions would be futile.) Ingersoll goes on that Grenville "said he did not think any body here [i.e., in his government] was furnished with Materials for that purpose." In any event, Grenville must go forward with his plan. "Upon the whole he said he had pledged his Word for Offering the Stamp Bill to the house, that the house would hear all our Objections & would do as they thought best." Just as they did after the meeting in May 1764, the agents left with no new information; they realized even more clearly that Grenville was committed to a bill for stamp duties.

Ingersoll, much more optimistic than Mauduit on January 16, closes with a positive view of the likely role of British merchants.

> The Merchants in London are alarmed at these things; they have had a meeting with the Agents & are about to petition Parliament upon the Acts that respect the trade of North America.[10]

Purpose of the Stamp Act: Right, not Revenue

The American protests were to provoke additional motivation for the stamp duties: demonstration of the right to levy taxes on the colonies. When Whately wrote Temple on November 5, 1764, the motivation for stamp duties had been revenue.

> Burthen'd as this country is with debt and with expence, some attention must be had to revenue, and the Colonies must contribute their share; tho' I believe, as there is no idea of charging them very highly, the part they will bear will be found much less than their proportion.[11]

Only three months later, the act then under consideration in the House of Commons, the motive was quite different.

> The great measure of the Sessions is the American Stamp Act; I give it the Appellation of a great Measure on account of *the important point it establishes, the right of Parliament to lay an internal Tax upon the Colonies.* We wonder here that it ever was doubted. There is not a single member of Parliament to be found that will dispute it.[12]

As more American refusals to recognize the authority of Parliament came to light, the need to establish the right to levy the tax became ever more important. The reaction of British leaders is shown by this letter of February 14 from Edward Sedgwick (a knowledgeable undersecretary of state) to a colleague.

> What you have heard of the Refractoriness of the Colonies is very true. There are several Resolutions of American Assemblies, in which they almost deny or strongly remonstrate against the Right of the Parliament to tax them, which are directed by Order in Council to be laid before the Parliament. But first it is thought proper to establish that Right by a new execution of it, and in the strongest instance, an internal Tax, that of the Stamp Duty.[13]

Four

The Stamp Act

> "The great measure of the Sessions is the American Stamp Act; I give it the Appellation of a great Measure on account of the important point it establishes, the right of Parliament to lay an internal Tax upon the Colonies."
>
> —Thomas Whately, February 1765

THE DESIRE TO establish parliamentary supremacy over the colonies on top of the need for revenue led to easy passage of the Stamp Act. There was never a question of the right of Parliament to levy such a tax nor was there disagreement about the justice of the colonies being taxed to contribute toward the upkeep of British troops for their defense.

In Ingersoll's letter to Governor Fitch (of February 11, 1765), he described the attitude of British leaders.

> The principal Attention has been to the Stamp bill that has been preparing to Lay before Parliament for taxing America. The Point of the Authority of Parliament to impose such Tax I found on my Arrival here was so fully and Universally yielded, that there was not the least hopes of making any impressions that way.

> Indeed, it has appeared since that the House would not suffer to be brought in, nor would any one Member Undertake to Offer to the House, any Petition from the Colonies that held forth ye Contrary of that Doctrine.

He provides "a Summary of the Arguments which are made Use of in favour of such Authority."

> The House of Commons, say they, is a branch of the supreme legislature of the Nation. . . . They further urge, that the only reason why America has not been heretofore taxed in the fullest Manner, has been merely on Account of their infancy and inability . . . and they deny any Distinction between what is called an internal & external Tax as to the point of the Authority imposing such taxes.

Charters have no standing because "the King cannot grant any that shall exempt [the colonies] from the Authority of one of the branches of the great body of Legislation."

> In short they say *a Power to tax is a necessary Part of every Supreme Legislative Authority,* and that if they have not that Power over America, they have none, & then America is at once a Kingdom of itself.[1]

Passage

Parliament opened on January 10, but little attention was paid to the colonies until February 6. Grenville introduced the resolutions that defined the planned taxation.

> [1] Resolved, That it is the Opinion of this Committee, That a Stamp Duty of Three Pence, Sterling Money, be charged upon every Skin or Piece of Vellum or Parchment, or Sheet or Piece of Paper, on which shall be ingrossed, written or printed, any Declaration, Plea, Replication, Rejoinder, Demurrer, or other Pleading, or any Copy thereof, in any Court of Law within the British colonies and Plantations in America.

There were fifty-five resolutions, all but the last stating the duties to be levied; the last stating the purpose of the revenue, "further defraying the necessary Expences of defending, protecting, and securing, the said Colonies and Plantations."[2]

Grenville begins by explaining his reason for delay from the previous year.[3]

> The reason of the delaying the proposal to this year was to gain all possible information and to give Americans an opportunity of conveying information to this House, whose ears are always open to receive knowledge and to act to it.

He gives no serious consideration to colonial protests that disputed the right of taxation. He "wished now to avoid that question" because "no person can doubt it." He also points out the danger of the colonial objections, that they deny more than just taxation: "The objection of the colonies is from the general right of mankind not to be taxed but by their representatives. This goes to all laws in general."

But he nonetheless makes the case that the colonies are represented: "The Parliament of Great Britain virtually represents the whole Kingdom. . . . Not a twentieth part of the people are actually represented." He dismisses the protests of the colonies, first giving no credit to the assertions of right made by the proprietary and charter colonies, then rejecting the rationale of the royal colonies in a single sentence as having power only "to make general laws, according to the custom of England." He gives precedents for taxation by Parliament, then stresses the urgency of acting. Failure to pass the tax after the colonies have protested would set a precedent and would function as acknowledgment that Parliament did not have authority to levy such a tax. "If we reject this proposition now, we shall declare that we ought not to tax the colonies."

> While they remain dependent, they must be subject to our legislature. . . . They have in many instances encroached and claimed powers and privileges inconsistent with their situation

> as colonies. *If they are not subject to this burden of tax, they are not entitled to the privilege of Englishmen.*

He ends with the principle of reciprocity: "This law is founded on the great maxim that protection is due from [those who govern], and support and obedience on the part of the governed."

William Beckford, one of America's allies in opposition to taxation, "admits right of taxing the imports and exports of the colonies, and . . . the colonies all admit this principle." But internal taxation is objectionable: "The North Americans do not think an internal and external duty the same." He turns to the situation in Great Britain: "As to representation, all England is not represented, but it is a written part of our constitution that it is so." Beckford ends with a motion for the "Chairman to leave the Chair," a procedural device to avoid a vote on the resolutions, with the effect that the resolutions would not be approved. The motion is the basis for all remaining debate.

Sir William Meredith points out that the proposed taxation is inappropriate because neither the members nor their constituents are subject to the tax.

> The safety of this country consists in this with respect that we cannot lay a tax upon others without taxing ourselves. This is not the case in America. We shall tax them in order to ease ourselves. We ought therefore to be extremely delicate in imposing a burden upon others which we not only do not share ourselves but which is to take it far from us.

Rose Fuller, a West Indian planter, "Admits the right but doubts the propriety of laying this tax. Is afraid of the discord and confusion which it may produce."

The next section of the debate is best told in the letter of February 11 from Ingersoll to Fitch. It contains a report of a stirring speech that makes Colonel Isaac Barre popular in America. Barre had served in the colonies during the French and Indian War—wounded and lost an eye at the battle for Quebec—and was a consistent supporter of the American cause. First, Ingersoll reports the speech to which Barre responded.

> Charles Townsend spoke in favour of the Bill . . . and concluded with the following or like Words. And now will these Americans, Children planted by our Care, nourished up by our Indulgence untill they are grown to a Degree of Strength & Opulence, and protected by our Arms, will they grudge to contribute their mite to releive us from the heavy weight of that burden which we lie under?

In response, "Mr. Barre rose and [addressed the] Concluding words of Mr. Townshend, and in a most spirited & I thought an almost inimitable manner, said,"

> They planted by your Care? No! Your Oppressions planted em in America. They fled from your Tyranny to a then uncultivated and unhospitable Country, where they exposed themselves to almost all the hardships to which human Nature is liable.
>
> They nourished up by your indulgence? They grew by your neglect of Em; as soon as you began to care about Em, that Care was Excercised in sending persons to rule over Em, in one Department and another, who were perhaps the Deputies of Deputies to some Member of this house—sent to Spy out their Lyberty, to misrepresent their Actions & to prey upon Em; men whose behaviour on many Occasions has caused the Blood of those *Sons of Liberty* to recoil within them.
>
> They protected by your Arms? they have nobly taken up Arms in your defence, have Exerted a Valour amidst their constant & Laborious industry for the defence of a Country, whose frontier, while drench'd in blood, its interior Parts have yielded all its little Savings to your Emolument. And beleive me, remember I this Day told you so, that same Spirit of freedom which actuated that people at first, will accompany them still.—But prudence forbids me to explain myself further. God

> knows I do not at this Time speak from motives of party Heat, what I deliver are the genuine Sentiments of my heart.[4]

The resulting debate went on for hours with many speakers opposing the act; but there was no significant assertion that such taxation was beyond the rightful authority of Parliament. Despite the number of speakers opposed, Grenville had the votes. Beckford's motion was defeated at 8 p.m., 245 to 49. The result was decisive, Whately later writing Temple that "this puts an end to all opposition to the principle of the bill, & now the rates are the only question."[5] After the division, the committee took two hours to approve the remaining resolutions. All fifty-five were quietly approved by the house the next day.

On February 8, Charles Garth wrote the committee of correspondence of South Carolina.

> [On February 6, Grenville] proposed to the Committee of Ways and Means, the measure the House thought might be proper and necessary: that of charging certain Stamp Duties in America. The arguments urg'd tended to prove that the Colonies were all virtually represented in Parliament in the same manner as those of the subjects of Great Britain who did not vote for representatives. Sundry Acts of Parliament were recited that had from time to time been enacted imposing duties on the American subjects [and] that there could not be a distinction between powers of legislation and taxation.

Grenville emphasized that the colonies would not be burdened by the tax and that the colonies had relatively few debts,

> all of which were to be paid off before the year 1769, that therefore it was but reasonable the Colonies should contribute at least to take off that part of the burthen from the Mother Country which concerned the protection and defence of themselves.

Garth goes on that, "the power of Parliament was asserted and so universally agreed to, that no petition disputing it will be received." He reports the lopsided division (245 to 49), himself in the minority. He intends to submit a modest petition for South Carolina that he hopes will not offend Parliament. But "what the success of the petitions that can be presented will be, the division above mentioned will, I fear, but too fully prepare you."[6]

The second reading of the bill on February 15 largely dealt with colonial petitions, only three being presented. One petition was prepared by Garth, another by the agent of Virgina (Montague) and—the only petition prepared in the colonies—that of Connecticut. For each of the three petitions, on a motion "that the said Petition be brought up; it passed in the Negative." Arguments for hearing the petitions were made along these lines: "The postponing of the Bill last year was to give the colonies time to petition, if they thought proper. They had too a peculiar right to do so, as not being represented." Grenville counterargued: "Totally denies the fact. It was postponed to give time for information not for opposition. Denies their not being represented. As much so, as the greater part of the people of England."[7]

Garth explained the British rationale. A motion to bring up the Virginia petition was seconded by him, "thereupon a debate arose whether to receive or reject it." The policy was "unquestion'd not to admit petitions against a Money Bill." But there was more than a question of procedure. "This was not the sole reason that determin'd the fate of the petitions that were offer'd."

> The House declared they would not suffer a petition that should hint at questioning the supremacy and authority of Parliament to impose taxes in every part of the British Dominions. The debate ended with the question put for leave to bring up the petition, which was carry'd in the negative.

He discusses other petitions.

> Some of the petitions that were framed in America and sent over from some of the Colonies to their agents questioned the

> power of Parliament in very high tones, phrases inserted that Members very well inclin'd to serve the Colonies could not be prevailed with to offer them to the House from a certainty of incurring the censure of Parliament.

He also comments on the nature of instructions to the agents.

> Those of the Colonies who had not transmitted petitions of their own penning, have all in their instructions expressed themselves upon this head in such manner, that petitions could not well be drawn by those agents to the satisfaction of their constituents without [offending Parliament].

The modest petition he prepared for South Carolina suffered the same fate as others.

> Notwithstanding the fate of the Virginia petition I determin'd to offer mine on the part of S. Carolina, and accordingly mov'd to bring it up; I was call'd upon to state the contents, which done, the House were of opinion it tended to question the right of Parliament to exercise this power of taxation, and being likewise against a Money Bill, was also refus'd.[8]

Ingersoll wrote Fitch on March 6, providing more detail about the results of the petitions. The Virginia petition "implied their denial of the right of Parliament to tax the Colonies. This drew on a pretty warm debate. . . . I think no-body but General Conway denied the right of Parliament to tax us." More debate followed.

> [Except for] Gentlemen Interested in ye West Indies & a few Members [that] happen to be Particularly connected with some of the colonies & a few of the [opposition faction] who are sure to athwart & oppose ye Ministry . . . there are Scarce any People here, Either within Doors or Without, but what approve the Measures now taking which Regard America.

When the question was put to receive the petition, it failed "by a great Majority. Then Mr. Jackson offered ours [Connecticut] which met with the same Fate." Regarding Massachusetts, Jackson announced "he had one to offer" but seeing how things were going "he told the house he would defer it till another Time." No member was willing to introduce the New York petition, "conceived in terms so inflammatory that he [New York agent Robert Charles] could not prevail on any one Member of the House to present it."[9]

Writing on June 12, Whately explained the British attitude about the petitions.

> With us there is not a difference of opinion. The House of Commons would not receive any petitions, however expressed, that implied a doubt of the right of Parliament to lay taxes. To receive the petitions would have been an acknowledgment that ye right was questionable, which we cannot admit.[10]

The bill was amended (February 18, 19, and 21) in several ways, the most important—and controversial—being an extension of the jurisdiction of courts of admiralty. Grenville received advice against such extension when he asked Charles Yorke, former (and future) attorney general, to review the bill. Yorke submitted a report on February 17 asserting that courts of record in the colonies could be trusted with jurisdiction, that most American vice-admiralty courts were "paultry & corrupt," and that the respectable court at Halifax, Nova Scotia (home port for the British fleet in America) was too far away. Furthermore, "the stamp duties have nothing of a maritime or commercial nature."[11]

The third reading of the bill in the House of Commons on February 27 was a formality, the bill being passed without a division. The Lords passed the bill on March 8 without debate; it received the royal assent on March 22, 1765.[12]

Abridged Text of the Act

The full text of the act runs to twenty-five closely printed pages (more than half of which deal with its administration). In broad outline, the act levies taxes for licenses and diplomas; leases, contracts, and bills of sale; pamphlets, handbills, and newspapers; and most legal documents used in court proceedings. All such documents were required to be prepared on material—vellum, parchment, or paper—prestamped by the newly-established American Stamp Office in London. Paper had to be purchased from a stamp distributor, the price including the cost of the paper and the appropriate tax. The act spelled out penalties for public officials recording unstamped documents, for lawyers proceeding in a suit without stamped paper, for selling unstamped newspapers, and for other failures to use stamped paper.

The title and preamble lay out the intent of the act.[13]

> An act for granting and applying certain stamp duties, and other duties, in the British colonies and plantations in America, towards further defraying the expences of defending, protecting, and securing the same; and for amending such parts of the several acts of parliament relating to the trade and revenues of the said colonies and plantations, as direct the manner of determining and recovering the penalties and forfeitures therein mentioned.

The preamble.

> Whereas it is just and necessary, that provision be made for raising a further revenue within your Majesty's dominions in America, towards defraying the said expences: we, your Majesty's most dutiful and loyal subjects, the commons of Great Britain in parliament assembled, have therefore resolved to give and grant unto your Majesty the several rates and duties herein after mentioned. . . . That from and after [November 1, 1765] there shall be raised, levied, collected, and paid unto his Majesty.

The preamble continues for eight pages of specific rates of duty—all payable in British sterling money, not colonial currency.

> For every skin or piece of vellum or parchment, or sheet or piece of paper, on which shall be ingrossed, written or printed, any declaration, plea, replication, rejoinder, demurrer, or other pleading, or any copy thereof, in any court of law within the British colonies and plantations in America, a stamp duty of three pence.

Despite the statement "any court," the duties were placed on papers used in civil courts, having no effect on criminal courts.

The preamble goes on to specify over forty rates beginning "For every skin or piece of vellum or parchment or sheet or piece of paper, on which shall be ingrossed, written, or printed,"

> any special bail and appearance upon such bail in any such court, a stamp duty of two shillings.
> any petition, bill, answer, claim, plea, replication, rejoinder, demurrer, or other pleading in any court of chancery or equity within the said colonies and plantations, a stamp duty of one shilling and six pence.
> any copy of any petition, bill, answer, claim, plea, replication, rejoinder, demurrer, or other pleading in any such court, a stamp duty of three pence.
> any monition, libel, answer, allegation, inventory, or renunciation in ecclesiastical matters in any court of probate, court of the ordinary, or other court exercising ecclesiastical jurisdiction within the said colonies and plantations, a stamp duty of one shilling.

(That mention of "ecclesiastical jurisdiction" alarmed those who followed non-Anglican religions that there were future plans for establishment of the Church of England.)

> any degree taken in any university, academy, college, or seminary of learning, within the said colonies and plantations.
> any monition, libel, claim, answer, allegation, information, letter of request, execution, renunciation, inventory, or other pleading, in any admiralty court.

There are a number of employment-related duties included.

> For every . . . licence, appointment, or admission of any counsellor, solicitor, attorney, advocate, or proctor, to practice in any court, or of any notary.

The act taxed papers dealing with shipping, thereby affecting merchants and external commerce.

> For every . . . note or bill of lading, which shall be signed for any kind of goods, wares, or merchandize, to be exported from, or any cocket or clearance.
> any licence for retailing of spirituous liquors.
> any indenture, lease, conveyance, contract, stipulation, bill of sale, protest, articles of apprenticeship, or covenant.

In addition, "and for and upon every pack of playing cards, and all dice." There follows a long statement of stamp duties based on usage of paper (e.g., "larger than half a sheet, and not exceeding one whole sheet"). Such duties were generally thought to be very high and damaging to printers.

> And for and upon every paper, commonly called a pamphlet, and upon every newspaper, containing publick news, intelligence, or occurrences, which shall be printed, dispersed, and made publick, within any of the said colonies and plantations, and for and upon such advertisements as are herein after mentioned, the respective duties.
> For every such pamphlet and paper contained in half a sheet, or and lesser piece of paper, which shall be so printed.

There are additional duties affecting printers: "For every advertisement to be contained in any gazette, newspaper, or other paper, or any pamphlet which shall be so printed. . . . For every almanack or calendar, for any one particular year." The preamble ends with specification of duties related to "any clerk or apprentice, which shall be put or placed to or with any master or mistress to learn any profession, trade, or employment." The duties continue in section 2 with duties related to the salary of clerks and apprentices.

Sections 3-53 define procedures for collecting the revenue and penalties for evading the duties. They include issues related to insurance, rules and regulations, exceptions to the tax for certain purposes (e.g., exception to taxes on the will of a "common seaman or soldier"), designation of officers involved in administration, and the oath to be taken by such officers.

Section 54 specifies the fundamental purpose of the act, that is, the use of money collected as taxes.

> That all the monies which shall arise by the several rates and duties hereby granted . . . shall be paid into the receipt of his Majesty's exchequer, and shall be entered separate and apart from all other monies, and shall be there reserved to be from time to time disposed of by parliament, towards further defraying the necessary expences of defending, protecting, and securing, the said colonies and plantations.

Sections 55-63 prescribe further administrative procedures, including expanding the authority of courts of admiralty and specifying "That all sums of money granted and imposed by this act . . . shall be deemed and taken to be sterling money of Great Britain."

Implementation

Grenville took several actions related to implementation of the act. To deal with the appointment of stamp distributors he directed the American Stamp Office to appoint prominent colonists. According to Ingersoll, Grenville said that some Americans

> told him that we were poor & unable to bear such tax; others told him we were well able; now, says he, take ye business into your own hands; you will see how & where it pinches & will certainly let us know it, in which Case it shall be Eased.[14]

The office took care in making appointments, largely completed in April, May, and June (although delivery of appointments to the stamp distributors was inexplicably long delayed). Appointment as a stamp distributor, one for each colony, would be a position that was profitable and prestigious; prominent and knowledgeable Americans in London sought such positions (such as Ingersoll) or advanced the cause of others (as Franklin did). That such colonists did not see the coming storm makes it understandable that the Grenville ministry and Parliament did not see that the protests of 1764 (so cavalierly rejected thought many Americans) would later transform into violent resistance.

Section 54 of the act (money to be paid into the exchequer) was a major concern of the Americans, but Grenville had no desire to remove specie from the colonies. After passage of the act, he took administrative action, ordering that the revenue (and also revenue from the Sugar Act) be handed over to the deputy paymasters in the colonies. Whately described the solution and its effect.

> The whole money to be raised is appropriated to the defence of the Colonies, & will consequently never be drawn out of them; so that the only effect of the tax will be that we shall send so much less than we have hitherto, & after all we shall still send by much the greater part of the money required for that purpose, & more than we did during ye last peace.[15]

The plan was designed to avoid high freight and insurance rates to send specie back and forth. However, it did not address the problem that most of the money would be paid out in the frontier territories, not where the bulk of the money was to be collected.

PART TWO

Resistance

"The year 1765 has been the most remarkable year of my life. That enormous engine, fabricated by the British Parliament, for battering down all the rights and liberties of America, I mean the Stamp Act, has raised and spread through the whole continent a spirit that will be recorded to our honor with all future generations. In every colony, from Georgia to New Hampshire inclusively, the stamp distributers and inspectors have been compelled by the unconquerable rage of the people to renounce their offices.

The people, even to the lowest ranks, have become more attentive to their liberties, more inquisitive about them, and more determined to defend them, than they were ever before known or had occasion to be. . . . Our presses have groaned, our pulpits have thundered, our legislatures have resolved, our towns have voted; the crown officers have everywhere trembled, and all their little tools and creatures been afraid to speak and ashamed to be seen."

—John Adams diary, December 1765

Five

Denial

"The Taxation of the People by themselves, or by Persons chosen by themselves to represent them . . . is the only Security against a burthensome Taxation, and the distinguishing Characteristick of British Freedom."

—Virginia House of Burgesses, May 1765

ALTHOUGH THE AMERICANS were agitated and had made lengthy protests in 1764 about the planned stamp duties, the early months of 1765 were calm and quiet. An abstract of Grenville's fifty-five resolutions for stamp duties was published in Boston newspapers on April 8; all the resolutions were printed in the *Pennsylvania Gazette* on April 18. By early May news of the actual passage was widespread.[1] Starting midyear, colony after colony denied Parliament the right to tax them, elaborating on the constitutional objections first stated in 1764. The assemblies of nine colonies made formal resolutions, all with the meaning that it was "the undoubted Right of Englishmen, that no Taxes be imposed on them, but with their own Consent, given personally, or by their Representatives." There is much repetition in the resolves, a telling and retelling of the story that expresses a consensus position regarding parliamentary taxation.[2]

Virginia

The first act of resistance to the Stamp Act was the statement of the Virginia Burgesses, soon to be famous as the *Virginia Resolves*. How the resolves set off the colonial revolt—continent-wide resistance—is a complex story. It begins with this letter from Lieutenant Governor Fauquier to the Board of Trade on June 5.

> On Saturday, the first instant, I dissolved the Assembly. . . . The four Resolutions, which I now have the honor to inclose to your Lordships, will shew your Lordships the Reason of my Conduct, and I hope, justify it. I will relate the whole proceeding to your Lordships in as concise a manner as I am able.
>
> On Wednesday, the 29th of May just at the end of the Session, when most of the Members had left the town, there being but 39 present out of 116 of which the house of Burgesses now consists, a motion was made to take into Consideration the Stamp Act, a Copy of which had crept into the house, and in a Committee of the whole house five Resolutions were proposed and agreed to, all by very small majorities. On Thursday the 30th, they were reported and agreed to by the House, the numbers being as before in the Committee, the greatest majority being 22 to 17, for the 5th 20 to 19 only.
>
> On Friday the 31st there having happened a small alteration in the house, there was an attempt to strike all the Resolutions off the Journals. The 5th which was thought the most offensive was accordingly struck off, but it did not succeed as to the other four.

The "other four," were not offensive, being not much more than a paraphrase of the Virginia petitions at the end of 1764. But the story deepens.

> I am informed the Gentlemen had two more resolutions in their pocket, but finding the difficulty they had in carrying the 5th which was by a single Voice, and knowing them to be more virulent and inflammatory, they did not produce them.

Fauquier could not suspect that the resolution "struck off" and the two "in their pocket" would later gain wide visibility in newspapers as though they were the formal position of the colony.

> The most strenuous opposers of this rash heat were the late Speaker, the King's Attorney and Mr. Wythe; but they were overpowered by the Young, hot, and Giddy Members. In the Course of the debates I have heard that very indecent language was used by a Mr. Henry, a young Lawyer who had not been a Month a Member of the House, who carried all the young Members with him; so that I hope I am authorized in saying there is cause at least to doubt whether this would have been the Sense of the Colony if more of their Representatives had done their Duty by attending to the end of the Session.[3]

The four agreed resolutions are printed in the *Journals of the House of Burgesses*.

> [1] That the first Adventurers and Settlers of this his Majesty's Colony and Dominion of Virginia brought with them, and transmitted to their Posterity, and all other his Majesty's Subjects since inhabiting in this his Majesty's said Colony, all the Liberties, Privileges, Franchises, and Immunities, that have at any Time been held, enjoyed, and possessed, by the people of Great Britain.
> [2] That by two royal Charters, granted by King James the First, the Colonists aforesaid are declared entitled to all Liberties, Privileges, and Immunities of Denizens and natural Subjects, to all Intents and Purposes, as if they had been abiding and born within the Realm of England.
> [3] That the Taxation of the People by themselves, or by Persons chosen by themselves to represent them, who can only know what Taxes the People are able to bear, or the easiest Method of raising them, and must themselves be affected by every Tax laid on the People, is the only Security against a burthensome Taxation, and the distinguishing Characteristick of

British Freedom, without which the ancient Constitution cannot exist.

[4] That his Majesty's liege People of this his most ancient and loyal Colony have without Interruption enjoyed the *inestimable Right of being governed by such Laws respecting their internal Polity and Taxation as are derived from their own Consent*, with the Approbation of their Sovereign, or his Substitute; and that the same hath never been forfeited or yielded up, but hath been constantly recognized by the Kings and People of Great Britain.[4]

The fourth resolve provides an example of how the resolves of 1765 paraphrase the Virginia position in December 1764, in this case repeating a phrase used in the address to the king.

The first publication of the resolves was in the *Newport Mercury* of June 24 (copied in the Boston papers of July 1, then throughout the colonies). That first publication, and others that used it as a model, omitted the third resolution printed in the journals of the Burgesses but printed the resolution struck off on May 31 plus the two virulent and inflammatory resolutions never presented to the Burgesses. The resolutions were introduced with this preamble.

Whereas the Honorable House of Commons, in England, have of late drawn into question how far the General Assembly of this colony hath power to enact laws for laying of taxes and imposing duties payable by the People of this, his Majesty's most ancient colony; for settling and ascertaining the same to all future times, the House of Burgesses . . . have come to the following resolves.

This is an astounding assertion, that a colonial legislative body can settle an issue having to do with the authority of Parliament. The resolution that was "struck off" proclaims the taxation authority of Parliament to be unconstitutional.

[5] That the General Assembly of this colony . . . [has] the only

> exclusive right and power to lay taxes and imposts upon the inhabitants of this colony; and that every attempt to vest such power in any other person or persons whatever than the General Assembly aforesaid, is illegal, unconstitutional, and unjust, and has a manifest tendency to destroy British as well as American liberty.

The two resolutions never presented to the Burgesses advocate resistance to parliamentary taxation.

> That his majesty's liege people, the inhabitants of this colony, are not bound to yield obedience to any law or ordinance whatever, designed to impose any taxation whatsoever upon them, other than the laws or ordinances of the General Assembly aforesaid.
>
> That any person who shall, by speaking or writing, assert or maintain that any person or persons, other than the General Assembly of this colony, have any right or power to impose or lay any taxation on the people here, shall be deemed an enemy to his majesty's colony.[5]

The resolves, as published, set a high standard—and were often an exact model—for aggressive resolves of other colonies. They were never published in the *Virginia Gazette*, the Williamsburg newspaper, being thought by the editor to be too radical.

The resolves quickly prompted action in other colonies. Governor Bernard wrote on July 20 that the *Newport Mercury* had reached Boston late in June, and the "Spirit of Rebellion" of the resolves had "roused up the Boston Politicians." On August 15, he wrote "the Virginia Resolves proved an Alarm bell to the disaffected," prompting a violent protest in Boston against the Stamp Act. And in September, General Thomas Gage—commander in chief of the British armed forces in North America, headquartered in New York City—wrote that the resolves "gave the Signal for a general outcry over the Continent."[6]

Fauquier's letter of June 5 arrived in London on July 27. Likely as a result of his sanguine attitude—about this not being the true sense of the Burgesses—it raised little concern. The secretary of state on September 14 simply directed him to "preserve the peace and tranquillity of the province committed to your care." Fauquier responded on December 11 after violent resistance had erupted in every colony. He paints a picture of the desperate situation late in the year: "At the time the Resolutions were passed in a very thin House, I hoped a fuller house would have quashed them, but by what has since happened . . . I fear I was mistaken in that point. . . . At present the Colonies reciprocally inflame each other and where the Fury will stop I know not."[7]

Massachusetts

On May 30, Governor Bernard opened the session of the Massachusetts legislature with a speech to the General Assembly. He dealt with the Stamp Act, relating it to an expected reorganization of the colonies that "must necessarily produce some regulations, which, from their novelty only, will appear disagreeable. But I am convinced, and doubt not but experience will confirm it, that they will operate, as they are designed, for the benefit and advantage of the colonies. In the mean time a respectful submission to the decrees of the Parliament is their interest as well as their duty." He then states the need for such submission.

> In an empire, extended and diversified as that of Great Britain, *there must be a supreme legislature,* to which all other powers must be subordinate. It is our happiness that our supreme legislature, the Parliament of Great Britain, is the sanctuary of liberty and justice.[8]

There was no response from the assembly. "The house thought it a time for action, rather than speculation; and, contrary to usual practice, suffered the speech to pass without any address, or notice of any sort."[9]

The assembly sent a circular letter dated June 8 to speakers of other colonial legislatures.

> The House of Representatives of this Province . . . propose a

> meeting . . . of the several British colonies on this continent, to consult together on the present circumstances of the colonies.

They called for "a general and united, dutiful and humble representation of their condition to his Majesty and the Parliament, to implore relief," proposing that "such meeting be at the city of New York, on the first Tuesday of October next."[10] The proposal resulted in a meeting of representatives from nine colonies, now known as the Stamp Act Congress.

On July 8, Bernard wrote to the Board of Trade about the proposed meeting.

> It was impossible to oppose this Measure to any good purpose: and therefore the friends of Government took the lead in it, & have kept it in their hands. . . . Of the Committee appointed by this house to meet the other Committees at New York on the first of Octr next, Two of the three are fast friends to Government & prudent & discreet men, such as I am assured will never consent to any undutiful or improper applications to the Government of great Britain.[11]

On September 25, following violent protests in August against the Stamp Act—in fact, riots in which mobs destroyed the Boston homes of several British officials and forced the appointed stamp distributor to resign—Bernard again addressed the General Assembly. Although he was not in favor of the Stamp Act (believing Parliament should leave raising internal taxes to the provincial legislatures) once the act was passed, he felt it necessary to demand its implementation.

> I have only to say, that it is an act of the Parliament of Great Britain, and as such ought to be obeyed by the subjects of Great Britain. And I trust that the supremacy of that Parliament, over all the members of their wide and diffused empire, never was and never will be denied within these walls.
>
> The right of the Parliament of Great Britain to make laws for the American colonies, however it has been controverted

> in America, remains indisputable at Westminster. If it is yet to be made a question, who shall determine it but the parliament? If the parliament declares that this right is inherent in them, are they likely to acquiesce [to] an open and forcible opposition to the exercise of it?

He distinguishes between right and expediency of taxing the colonies.

> It is said that the gentlemen who opposed this act in the house of commons [i.e., friends of the colonies], did not dispute the authority of parliament to make such a law, but argued upon the inexpediency of it at this time, and the inability of the colonies to bear such an imposition. These are two distinct questions, which may receive different answers. The power of the parliament to tax the colonies may be admitted, and yet the expediency of exercising that power at such a time, and in such a manner, may be denied.
>
> But if the questions are blended together, so as to admit of but one answer, the affirmation of the right of parliament will conclude for the expediency of the act.

He advises consideration that "if you found your application for relief upon denying the Parliament's right to make such a law, whether you will not take from your friends and advocates the use of those arguments which are most like to procure the relief you desire?"[12]

Meanwhile, back in London, the Grenville ministry had been dismissed (addressed in chapter 9). Bernard's first definite knowledge of the change in ministry came in a letter of September 25 from newly appointed secretary of state Henry Seymour Conway. On September 28, Bernard wrote Conway of his reason for the speech days earlier: "I had called the General Assembly to meet at Boston the 25th inst to try if I could get the assistance of the Legislature to carry the stamp Act into execution."[13]

The assembly answered Bernard on October 23, demonstrating the spirit restrained a year earlier when under pressure to compromise with Hutchinson and the council.

> You are pleased to say that the stamp act is an act of Parliament, and as such ought to be observed. This House, sir, has too great a reverence for the supreme legislature of the nation, to question its just authority. It by no means appertains to us to presume to adjust the boundaries of the power of Parliament; but boundaries there undoubtedly are.

The Massachusetts charter *does* set boundaries.

> Furthermore, your Excellency tells us that the right of the Parliament to make laws for the American colonies remains indisputable in Westminster. Without contending this point, we beg leave just to observe that the charter of the province invests the General Assembly with the power of making laws for its internal government and taxation; and that this charter has never yet been forfeited.

Inherent rights set further boundaries, representation being of particular significance.

> The Parliament has a right to make all laws [only] within the limits of their own constitution. Your Excellency will acknowledge that there are certain original inherent rights belonging to the people, which the Parliament itself cannot divest them of, consistent with their own constitution: among these is the *right of representation in the same body which exercises the power of taxation*. There is a necessity that the subjects of America should exercise this power within themselves, otherwise they can have no share in that most essential right, for they are not represented in Parliament, and indeed we think it impracticable.[14]

Rhode Island

Rhode Island made resolves on September 9, the first colony to do so after Virginia, and partly adopting the exact phrasing of those published resolves.

> 3. That His Majesty's liege people of this colony have enjoyed the right of being governed by their own Assembly in the article of taxes and internal police; and that the same hath never been forfeited, or any other way yielded up; but hath been constantly recognized by the King and people of Britain.

Rhode Island is taking a stronger stance than in November 1764, no longer believing that Parliament can lay duties "at pleasure."

> 4. That, therefore, the General Assembly of this colony have, in their representative capacity, the only exclusive right to lay taxes and imposts upon the inhabitants of this colony; and that every attempt to vest such power in any person or persons, whatever, other than the General Assembly aforesaid, is unconstitutional, and hath a manifest tendency to destroy the liberties of the people of this colony.

The next resolution is based on the Virginia model (all but for the addition of the word *internal*), one of the published resolves that was not presented to the Burgesses.

> 5. That His Majesty's liege people, the inhabitants of this colony, are not bound to yield obedience to any law or ordinance designed to impose any internal taxation whatsoever upon them, other than the laws or ordinances of the General Assembly.

The last resolve is unique to Rhode Island in that it directs officials to disobey the Stamp Act.

> 6. That all the officers in this colony, appointed by the authority thereof, be and they are hereby, directed to proceed in the execution of their respective offices in the same manner as usual; and that this Assembly will indemnify and save harmless all the said officers, on account of their conduct, agreeably to this resolution.[15]

Pennsylvania

Pennsylvania made resolves on September 21.

> 3. That the inhabitants of this Province are entitled to all the Liberties, Rights and Privileges of his Majesty's Subjects in Great-Britain, or elsewhere, and that the Constitution of Government in this Province is founded on the *natural Rights of Mankind*, and the noble Principles of English Liberty, and therefore is, or ought to be, perfectly free.

Taxation only by consent:

> 4. That it is the inherent Birth-right, and indubitable Privilege, of every British Subject, to be taxed only by his Consent, or that of his legal Representatives in Conjunction with his Majesty, or his Substitutes.
> 5. That the only legal Representatives of the Inhabitants of this Province are the Persons they annually elect to serve as Members of Assembly.

Resolved therefore:

> 6. That the Taxation of the People of this Province by any other Persons whatsoever than such their Representatives in Assembly, is unconstitutional, and subversive of their most valuable Rights.[16]

The mood in Pennsylvania at this time is further illustrated by a letter from patriot leader Charles Thomson in Philadelphia to Benjamin Franklin. First is the Franklin letter of July 11 from London to which Thomson responds.

> Depend upon it my good Neighbour, I took every Step in my Power, to prevent the Passing of the Stamp Act. . . . But the Tide was too strong against us. The Nation was *provok'd by American Claims of Independance*, and all Parties join'd in resolveing by this Act to Settle the Point.

> We might as well have hinder'd the Suns setting. That we could not do. But since 'tis down, my Friend, and it may be long before it rises again, Let us make as good a Night of it as we can. We may still Light Candles.

It is clear that in the summer of 1765 Franklin had no idea of the staunch resistance soon to be shown by his fellow Americans. Thomson responded on September 24.

> The sun of liberty is indeed fast setting, if not down already in the American colonies. But I much fear instead of the candles you mention being lighted, you will hear of the works of darkness. . . . It is not property only we contend for. Our liberty and most essential privileges are struck at. . . . Violence will beget resentment, and provoke to acts never dreamt of.[17]

Other Colonies

Massachusetts, Maryland, Connecticut, South Carolina, New Jersey, and New York made resolutions later in the year. Georgia, North Carolina, Delaware, and New Hampshire made no separate resolutions but otherwise expressed solidarity with the denial of authority of Parliament to tax the colonies. The consensus opinion of the thirteen colonies is discussed in the following chapter.

Dulany Denies Taxation

In early October 1765, Daniel Dulany of Maryland, a prominent lawyer and member of the governor's council, published a widely read pamphlet (with multiple reprintings in the colonies and in London) entitled *Considerations on the Propriety of Imposing Taxes in the British Colonies, for the Purpose of Raising a Revenue, by Act of Parliament.*[18] Dulany refuted the concept of virtual representation of the colonies in Parliament and specified his idea of the proper relationship between Great Britain and the colonies. His thinking was consistent with the American resolutions that established limits on the authority of Parliament, but he added that the denial of Parliament's authority to tax the colonies was not inconsistent with continued colonial subordination to Great Britain.

> In the constitution of England . . . the granting of supplies [laying taxes] is deemed to be the province of the House of Commons as the representative of the people. All supplies are supposed to flow from their gift; and the other orders are permitted only to assent or reject generally, not to propose any modification, amendment, or partial alteration of it.

However, "in framing the late Stamp Act, the Commons acted in the character of representative *of the colonies*. . . . But what right had the Commons of Great Britain to be thus munificent at the expence of the commons of America?"

> The colonies claim the privilege, which is common to all British subjects, of being taxed only with their own consent given by their representatives, and all the advocates for the Stamp Act admit this claim. Whether, therefore, upon the whole matter the imposition of the stamp duties is a proper exercise of constitutional authority or not depends upon the single question, whether the Commons of Great Britain are virtually the representatives of the commons of America or not?
>
> The advocates for the Stamp Act admit, in express terms, that "the colonies do not choose members of Parliament," but they assert that "the colonies are virtually represented in the same manner with the nonelectors resident in Great Britain."

Dulany denied such virtual representation.

> [In Great Britain] the interests . . . of the nonelectors, the electors, and the representatives are individually the same, to say nothing of the connection among neighbors, friends, and relations. The security of the nonelectors against oppression is that their oppression will fall also upon the electors and the representatives.

The situation was different in the colonies.

> There is not that intimate and inseparable relation between the electors of Great-Britain and the inhabitants of the colonies . . .

> on the contrary, not a single actual elector in England might be immediately affected by a taxation in America.

Certainly not adversely affected, but perhaps the opposite.

> Moreover, even acts oppressive and injurious to the colonies in an extreme degree might become popular in England from the promise or expectation that the very measures which depressed the colonies would give ease to the inhabitants of Great Britain.

He concludes his dissection of virtual representation that since "the colonies are not actually represented by the Commons of Great Britain . . . then the principle of the Stamp Act must be given up as indefensible on the point of representation."

The denial of authority to tax does not deny the subordination of the colonies to Great Britain. In a proper relationship between Great Britain and the colonies "the subordination and dependence of the colonies may be preserved." Parliament's authority "may justly be exercised to secure or preserve their dependence whenever necessary for that purpose."

> But though the right of the superior to use the proper means for preserving the subordination of his inferior is admitted, yet it does not necessarily follow that he has a right to seize the property of his inferior when he pleases or to command him in everything; since, in the degrees of it, there may very well exist a dependency and inferiority, without absolute vassalage and slavery.

Subordination has bounds.

> When powers compatible with the relation between the superior and inferior have by express compact been granted to and accepted by the latter, and have been, after that compact, repeatedly recognized by the former . . . the authority of the superior can't properly interpose, for by the powers vested in the inferior is the superior limited.

Dulany points out that advocates for the Stamp Act contend "the duties upon any exports or imports are internal taxes" and further claim "that no distinction can be supported between one kind of tax and another, an authority to impose the one extending to the other." But that is a false equivalence.

> There is a clear and necessary distinction between an act imposing a tax for the *single purpose of revenue* and those acts which have been made for the regulation of trade and have produced some revenue in consequence of their effect and operation as regulations of trade.

A duty imposed for the single purpose of revenue is taxation. Duties for the regulation of trade are different. Even "if an *incidental revenue* should be produced . . . these are not therefore unwarrantable." They are within "the authority of the mother country to regulate the trade of the colonies." He concludes about taxation:

> A right to impose an internal tax on the colonies without their consent for the *single purpose of revenue is denied*, a right to regulate their trade without their consent is admitted. The imposition of a duty may in some instances be the proper regulation.

He concludes about subordination:

> I acknowledge dependence on Great Britain, but I can perceive a degree of it without slavery, and I disown all other.

After his primary arguments, he has a data-filled appendix in which he asserts that restrictions on trade distort colonial commerce and are equivalent to taxation.

> A law [i.e., implicitly referring to the Navigation Act] which restrains one part of the society from *exporting* its products to the most profitable market *in favor of another*, or obliges it to

> *import* the manufactures of one country that are dear, instead of those of another that are cheap, is effectually a tax.[19]

Dickinson Seeks a Solution

John Dickinson, a successful Delaware and Pennsylvania lawyer and politician, later known as the "penman of the revolution," wrote William Pitt on December 21.[20] Although politely phrased, the letter was a warning (an apt summary of the temper in America). It was written after the American denial of the authority of Parliament had gone beyond words. Violent actions and threats of harm to stamp distributors and other British officials had by this time prevented it from going into effect in any colony (as we shall see in chapter 8). At this late point in the controversy Britain had no alternative: if the Stamp Act was not repealed the Americans would go their own way.

Dickinson believed that the British needed to resolve the "greatest Cause of Discontent in the Colonies . . . the Imposition of Taxes." He recognized that opponents of repeal would claim "that Great Britain by repealing that act will tacitly acknowledge that she has no Right to tax the Colonies."

> If the Repeal should be construed as such an Acknowledgment, it will only be renouncing a Right, the Exercise of which can never be repeated without throwing the Colonies into Desperation. This I hope Great Britain will never do; and therefore she cannot lose anything by such a Renunciation.

But the colonists would not view repeal in such a light; they would see the act as a product of the previous ministry "not at all admired here," and it would "be regarded as the Correction of their Error." He goes on that the duties imposed by the Stamp Act "must be attended with great Inconveniences [to the colonies], and in the End must be equally injurious to them and to Great Britain."

> If this shall be thought by the Parliament too slight a Pretence for the repeal, and that their Authority may be wounded by such Condescension, I am afraid they cannot hereafter rely on the Affection of the Colonies.

The colonies were not demanding independence: "As long as a good Understanding prevails between the Mother Country and her Colonies, they will, as they now do, greatly love and revere her." In fact, "the Colonies will not aim at Independence unless excited by the Treatment they receive from Great Britain." He ends with a round of compliments to Pitt and declares that he could be the one to save the day for the British Empire, topping it all off with

> If it is possible to form a Plan of Policy that shall establish for Ages the Union of Great Britain and her Colonies, We think it may be expected from You.

Six

Stamp Act Congress

"It is inseparably essential to the Freedom of a People, and the undoubted Right of Englishmen, that no Taxes be imposed on them, but with their own Consent, given personally, or by their Representatives."

—Stamp Act Congress, October 1765

THE MASSACHUSETTS LETTER of June 8 proposing a meeting of the "several British colonies on this continent" fell on fertile ground. What is now known as the Stamp Act Congress, referred to at the time as "the congress at New York," convened on October 7 with twenty-seven delegates from nine colonies: Massachusetts, Rhode Island, Connecticut, New York, New Jersey, Pennsylvania, Delaware, Maryland, and South Carolina. The delegates to the congress leaned toward conservative rather than radical philosophy, committed to restoring the British/American relationship to what it was before the new imperial policy of 1763: they were not seeking independence. The congress established the consensus position of the colonies, most importantly making a definitive statement that denied any right in Parliament to levy taxes on the colonies.[1]

With delegates beginning to arrive, New York lieutenant governor Cadwallader Colden was prompted to write Secretary of State Conway on September 23.

> This meeting was kept secret from me till lately. I have in discourse discountenanced it as an illegal convention & inconsistent with the Constitution of the Colonies by which their several Governments are made distinct & independent of each other. Whatever plausible pretenses may be made for this meeting their real intentions may be dangerous.[2]

General Gage wrote Conway on October 12: the delegates "are of various Characters and opinions, but it's to be feared in general, that the Spirit of Democracy is strong amongst them." He points out the constitutional issue as seen by the Americans.

> The question is not of the inexpediency of the Stamp Act, but that it is unconstitutional, and contrary to their Rights, Supporting the Independency of the Provinces; and not Subject to the Legislative Power of Great Britain.

Oddly, he expresses optimism.

> It is impossible to say whether the Execution of the Stamp Act will meet with further Opposition; but from present Appearances there is Reason to Judge that it may be introduced without much Difficulty in several of the Colonys, and if it is began in some, that it will soon spread over the rest.[3]

Gage's optimism, the letter reaching London on November 15, played a role in slowing the British response to American resistance.

In the first order of business, the congress elected as chairman Timothy Ruggles of Massachusetts. Delegates then decided on the method of voting: each colony was to have a single vote.

Products of the Congress

There were four products of the congress: a declaration of rights and grievances, and appeals to king, Lords, and Commons.[4] We have seen rights and grievances put forth by colonial assemblies, but their being spelled out by the Stamp Act Congress established a consensus in America's position.

The Declaration

On October 19, the Congress "agreed to the following Declarations of the Rights and Grievances."

> I. That his Majesty's Subjects in these Colonies, owe the same Allegiance to the Crown of Great-Britain that is owing from his Subjects born within the Realm, and all due Subordination to that August Body the Parliament of Great-Britain.

The undefined "due subordination" was a compromise about what acknowledgment of parliamentary authority was appropriate. Despite the "subordination," the declarations define representation in such a way as to deny the authority of Parliament to tax the colonies.

> II. That his Majesty's Liege Subjects in these Colonies are entitled to all the inherent Rights and Liberties of his Natural born Subjects within the Kingdom of Great-Britain.

Declarations three and four link taxation and representation.

> III. That it is inseparably essential to the Freedom of a People, and the undoubted Right of Englishmen, that no Taxes be imposed on them, but with their own Consent, given personally, or by their Representatives.
>
> IV. That the People of these Colonies are not, and from their local Circumstances cannot be, Represented in the House of Commons in Great-Britain.

Declarations five and six deny parliamentary authority for taxation by emphasizing that taxation, being a gift, differs from legislation.

> V. That the only Representatives of the People of these Colonies are Persons chosen therein by themselves, and that no Taxes ever have been, or can be Constitutionally imposed on them, but by their respective Legislature.
> VI. That all Supplies to the Crown, being free Gifts of the People, it is unreasonable and inconsistent with the Principles and Spirit of the British Constitution for the People of Great-Britain to grant to his Majesty the Property of the Colonists.

Declarations seven and eight state that the admiralty court is unjust.

> VII. That Trial by Jury, is the inherent and invaluable Right of every British Subject in these Colonies.
> VIII. That the late Act of Parliament, entitled [the Stamp Act] and several other Acts, by extending the Jurisdiction of the Courts of Admiralty beyond its ancient Limits, have a manifest Tendency to subvert the Rights and Liberties of the Colonists.

Declarations nine through eleven address economic problems:

> IX. That the Duties imposed by several late Acts of Parliament, from the peculiar Circumstances of these Colonies, will be extremely Burthensome and Grievous; and from the scarcity of Specie, the Payment of them absolutely impracticable.
> X. That as the Profits of the Trade of these Colonies ultimately center in Great-Britain, to pay for the Manufactures which they are obliged to take from thence, they eventually contribute very largely to all Supplies granted there to the Crown.
> XI. That the Restrictions imposed by several late Acts of Parliament on the Trade of these Colonies will render them unable to purchase the Manufactures of Great-Britain.

General concerns were also addressed:

> XII. That the Increase, Prosperity, and Happiness of these Colonies, depend on the full and free Enjoyment of their Rights

> and Liberties, and an Intercourse with Great-Britain mutually Affectionate and Advantageous.
>
> XIII. That it is the Right of the British Subjects in these Colonies, to Petition the King, or either House of Parliament.
>
> Lastly, That it is the indispensable Duty of these Colonies . . . to procure the Repeal of the Act for granting and applying certain Stamp Duties, of all Clauses of any other Acts of Parliament whereby the Jurisdiction of the Admiralty is extended as aforesaid, and of the other late Acts for the Restriction of American Commerce.

The declarations were first printed in the *Providence Gazette* in March 1766 and quickly republished in other colonial newspapers.

APPEALS: KING, LORDS, COMMONS

The congress made three appeals: to the king and each house of Parliament. The heart of the address to the king is quite short.

> The invaluable Rights of Taxing ourselves, and Trial by our Peers, of which we implore your Majesty's Protection, are not, we most humbly conceive, Unconstitutional; but confirmed by the Great CHARTER of English Liberty.

The memorial to the House of Lords limits the degree of subordination.

> That his Majesty's Liege Subjects in his American Colonies, tho' they acknowledge a due Subordination to that August Body the British Parliament, are entitled, in the Opinion of your Memorialists, *to all the inherent Rights and Liberties of the Natives of Great-Britain.*

There is an appeal for taxation by consent:

> That your Memorialists also humbly conceive another of these essential Rights to be the Exemption from all Taxes, but such

> as are imposed on the People by the several Legislatures in these Colonies, which Right also they have, till of late, freely enjoyed.

After making a specific objection to "the Act for granting certain Stamp Duties" they move to economic issues.

> Your Memorialists (not waving their Claim to these Rights . . .) humbly Represent, That from the peculiar Circumstances of these Colonies, the Duties imposed by the aforesaid Act, and several other late Acts of Parliament, are extremely Grievous and Burthensome, and the Payment of the said Duties will very soon, for want of Specie, become absolutely impracticable; and that the Restrictions on Trade by the said Acts, will not only greatly distress the Colonies, but must be extremely detrimental to the Trade and true Interest of Great-Britain.

The petition to the House of Commons is of most significance, pointing out that "several late Acts of Parliament imposing divers Duties and Taxes . . . but above all the Act for granting and applying certain Stamp Duties, &c. in America, have fill'd them with the deepest Concern and Surprize."

> We most sincerely recognize our Allegiance to the Crown, and acknowledge all due Subordination to the Parliament of Great-Britain . . . but it is with most ineffable and humiliating Sorrow, that we find ourselves, of late, deprived of the Right of Granting our own Property for his Majesty's Service.

The recent taxation was unprecedented.

> Your Petitioners further shew, That the remote Situation, and other Circumstances of the Colonies, render it impracticable that they should be Represented, but in their respective subordinate Legislature; and they humbly conceive, that the Parliament, adhering strictly to the Principles of the Constitution,

> have never hitherto Tax'd any but those who were actually therein Represented; for this Reason, we humbly apprehend, they never have Tax'd Ireland, or any other of the Subjects without the Realm.
>
> But were it ever so clear, that the Colonies might in Law, be reasonably deem'd to be Represented in the Honourable House of Commons, yet we conceive that very good Reasons [demonstrate] . . . it would be for the real Interest of Great-Britain, as well as her Colonies, that the late Regulations should be rescinded, and the several Acts of Parliament imposing Duties and Taxes on the Colonies . . . should be Repeal'd.

Since the House of Commons is the prime mover in all acts of taxation, the congress uses this petition to buttress its case against the authority of Parliament to levy any tax on the colonies.

> It is also humbly submitted, Whether there be not a material Distinction in Reason and sound Policy, at least, between [on the one hand] the necessary Exercise of Parliamentary *Jurisdiction in general Acts*, for the Amendment of the Common Law, and the Regulation of Trade and Commerce through the whole Empire, and [on the other hand] the *Exercise of that Jurisdiction by imposing Taxes on the Colonies.*

Humble phrasing aside, there *is* a material distinction. The congress recognized parliamentary authority over general acts while the right to levy taxes was denied. The petition ends with a dutiful and humble request that "the Honourable House . . . take our distressed and deplorable Case into their serious Consideration" and take appropriate action.[5]

At the close of the congress (on October 24), since having no standing to petition Parliament:

> It is recommended by the Congress, to the several Colonies to appoint special agents for soliciting relief from their present grievances, and to unite their utmost interest and endeavors for that purpose.

SUBJECT OF COLONIAL RIGHTS

As the congress was struggling with the issue of what subordination may be "due," they had available a *Report of a Committee on the Subject of Colonial Rights*, drafted by William Samuel Johnson of Connecticut, a prominent political figure, later an agent for Connecticut.

> The power of imposing taxes upon a people without their consent, must in the end deprive them of their liberty, be such power in the hands of one, the few, or the many.

After listing reasons "to show that the late regulations should be rescinded and the late acts imposing duties and taxes in America repealed," the report dealt directly with the phrase "due subordination," ending with a significant limitation.

> Altho the due *Subordination* of the colonies to the Crown and Parliament [is acknowledged] . . . yet it is most humbly conceived that this subordination and dependency is sufficiently secured by the common law, by our allegiance, by the negative of the crown on the laws of most of the provinces, but above all by the general superintending power and authority of the whole empire indisputably lodged in that august body, the parliament of Great Britain, which authority is clearly admitted here, so far as in our circumstances is consistent with the enjoyment of our essential rights as freemen and British subjects.

The report also added meaning to the distinction between legislation and taxation that was later adopted in the petition to the House of Commons; the wording used by Johnson more directly states what is acceptable and what is not. In addition, the report objected to both "external and internal duties and taxes," shortened in the official products of the congress to the single word "taxes."

> It is also submitted whether there is not a vast difference between the exercise of parliamentary *jurisdiction in general acts*

> for the amendment of the common law, *or even in* general regulations of trade and commerce through the empire, and the actual *exercise of that jurisdiction in levying external and internal duties and taxes on the colonists*, while they neither are nor can be represented in parliament.
>
> The former may very well consist with a reasonable measure of civil liberty in the colonies, but we must beg leave to say that how the latter is consistent with any degree of freedom we are wholly at a loss to comprehend.[6]

These ideas led to the conclusion that "due subordination" is subordination to legislation "consistent with the enjoyment of our essential rights" but not to taxation.

APPROVAL

The delegates from six colonies approved the products of the congress and signed the appeal: Massachusetts, Rhode Island, New Jersey, Pennsylvania, Delaware, and Maryland. The assemblies of Connecticut, New York, and South Carolina had not authorized their delegates to sign products of the congress. Signing after adjournment of the congress were Connecticut, South Carolina, and New Hampshire and Georgia (even though they did not attend). New York took strong independent action, consistent with the position of the congress but making its own resolves and petitions. The governors of North Carolina and Virginia did not convene the legislature until long after the Stamp Act had been repealed. On November 6, 1766, the North Carolina assembly criticized its governor for not meeting during the crisis. The earlier Virginia Resolves left no doubt as to where she stood.

Approval of the constitutional position taken by the congress was universal. Several colonies took additional actions in support, publishing additional resolves and often signing the three appeals and sending them to their agents in London. In total, ten colonies signed the appeals, all but for New York, Virginia, and North Carolina.[7]

Actions After the Congress

The products of the congress were not the final word. Several states, most dramatically New York, felt they had something extra to say.

Connecticut

On October 25, 1765, the Connecticut General Assembly approved the three appeals of the congress, sending them to agent Richard Jackson with instructions not to avoid the matter of right, but to insist upon it. "The power lately exercised by Parliament . . . is inconsistent with the principles and spirit of the British constitution." Therefore "we can by no means be content that you should give up the matter of right, but . . . [must] firmly insist upon the exclusive right of the Colonies to tax themselves."[8] Connecticut stated it most directly, but all the colonies insisted that their agents address "the matter of right." Such a stance forbade the agents from praying for repeal of the Stamp Act on economic grounds. Such an appeal would likely have found considerable support in the House of Commons, but such an appeal would have been tantamount to admitting the right of Parliament to levy a tax on the colonies.

The assembly produced their own set of resolves.

> 5. That his Majesty's liege subjects of this Colony have enjoyed the right and priviledge of being governed by their General Assembly in the article *of taxing and internal police*, agreeable to the powers and priviledges granted and contained in the royal charter . . . and that the same have never been forfeited or any way yielded up, but have been constantly recognized by the King and Parliament of Great Britain.

Both taxes and duties (for revenue) are special forms of legislation: a free gift. This is a turnabout from the position of Connecticut stated in October 1764, objecting only to internal taxation.

> 6. That, in the opinion of this House, an act for raising money by *duties or taxes* differs from other acts of legislation, in that it is always considered as a free gift of the people made by their

> *legal and elected representatives*; and that we cannot conceive that the people of Great Britain, or their representatives, have right to dispose of our property.[9]

Massachusetts

On October 29, the Massachusetts House of Representatives stated resolutions further showing their staunch opposition to taxation. The resolutions were from the assembly only but were authoritative. Massachusetts having approved the products of the congress was tantamount to rejecting the weak petition of November 1764, recanting the plea of privilege and making these statements their formal position.

> 1. Resolved, That there are certain essential rights of the British Constitution of Government, which are founded in the Law of God and nature, and are the common rights of mankind—Therefore
> 2. Resolved, That the inhabitants of this province are unalienably entitled to those essential rights in common with all men: and that no law of society can consistent with the law of god and nature, divest them of those rights.

Based on that foundation, the assembly denied the taxation authority of Parliament.

> 12. Resolved, As a just conclusion . . . that all acts made by any power whatever, other than the General Assembly of this province, imposing taxes on the inhabitants, are infringements of our inherent and unalienable rights, as men and British subjects: and render void the most valuable declarations of our charter.[10]

New York as a Special Case

New York agreed with the spirit of the declarations of the congress but chose to make an individual protest rather than approve and forward the products of the congress. On December 11, the assembly adopted petitions to king, Lords, and Commons.

In the petition to the House of Commons, after vowing "all due Submission to the supreme Authority of the British Legislature" they "beg Leave in duty to our Constituents, to petition against internal Taxes and Duties on merchandize for raising a revenue in this Colony." They restated the process of taxation in Great Britain.

> All parliamentary Aids in Great-Britain, are the *free Gifts of the People by their Representatives*, consented to by the Lords, and accepted by the Crown, and therefore every Act imposing them, essentially differs from every other Statute, having the Force of a Law in no other Respect than the Manner thereby prescribed for levying the Gift.

That is the distinction between taxes (free gifts from the people represented, the people of Great Britain) and other acts.

> That agreeable to this Distinction, the House of Commons has always contended for and enjoyed the constitutional Right of originating all Money Bills.

The House of Commons cannot do so for the unrepresented people of the colonies.

> That all Supplies to the Crown being in their Nature free Gifts, it would, as we humbly conceive, be unconstitutional for the People of Great-Britain, by their Representatives in Parliament, to dispose of the Property of Millions of his Majesty's Subjects, who are not, and cannot be there represented.[11]

The assembly passed resolutions on December 18. In the preamble they expressed "submission to the supreme legislative power," but such submission is limited by this resolve.

> Resolved. That they owe obedience to all acts of Parliament not inconsistent with the essential rights and liberties of Englishmen, and are intituled to the same rights and liberties which

> his majesty's English subjects, both within and without the realm, have ever enjoyed.

The final resolve contains a modest threat.

> Resolved. That if the honorable house of Commons insist on their power of taxing this colony, and by that means deprive its inhabitants of what they have always looked upon as an undoubted right, though this power should be exerted in the mildest manner, it will teach them to consider the people of Great Britain as vested with absolute power to dispose of all their property, and tend to weaken that affection for the mother country, which this colony ever had, and is extremely desirous of retaining.[12]

Seven

Nonimportation

"That in all orders they send out to Great Britain for goods or merchandise of any nature, kind, or quality whatsoever, usually imported from Great Britain, they will direct their correspondents not to ship them unless the Stamp Act be repealed."
—Agreement of New York Merchants, October 1765

NONIMPORTATION—a boycott of British manufactured goods in protest against the Stamp Act—was formally established in late 1765 as a threat intended to put pressure on British merchants and manufacturers. Before that point was reached, starting in 1764, individual merchants reduced imports from Great Britain as a consequence of economic hardship caused by the end of the Seven Years' War and the disruption caused by strict enforcement of the laws of trade (the vigorous enforcement of the Molasses Act and the even more onerous rules and regulations of the Sugar Act). In addition, the restrictions of the Currency Act—preventing paper bills of credit from being declared a legal tender—limited the medium of exchange necessary to carry on business.[1] (The effect of reduced trade on Great Britain is addressed in chapter 10.)

Distress of the Merchants

On June 22, 1764, Philadelphia merchant Samuel Rhoades Jr. wrote his London agents Neate, Pigou & Booth.

> I need not say much of future Dealings, because I fear that all our Trade with you must come to an End, for nothing can be more certain than its Intirely ceasing if your Legislature will carry into Execution those Resolves formed by the Committee of the whole House of Commons. . . . If we are not on any Terms allow'd a Trade to get Money from abroad, we shall have none to pay you for Goods, & then unless you will send them Gratis our Dealings must end.[2]

William Allen, the chief justice of Pennsylvania, wrote Barclay & Sons in London on November 20.

> No doubt you will hear fully of the low Ebb of Trade, which is distressed exceedingly. . . . Such Measures will soon make us poor, but our Creditors in England will suffer with us. We must learn Frugality and make all our necessaries ourselves, for we shall soon not be able to get them any other way, as our Money is gone, and our Credit will soon be at an end.

He wrote again on December 19.

> Our Money is yearly sinking . . . owing to the Act of Parliament passed last winter, which lays so many Difficulties upon our Trade . . . that it will be scarce possible to make Remittances, which I can, without a Gift of Prophecy, say, *will soon be perceived by the London Merchts & by all the Manufacturers in England.*[3]

Merchant anxiety increased in 1765. John Hancock, a wealthy merchant and one of the leading patriots of Boston, wrote a series of letters to his London agents Barnards & Harrison that illustrate the increasingly fraught situation of American merchants. On January 21, he expressed his concern over the depression in New England.

> [There is] great uneasiness and Losses here owing to the failure of some Persons of note . . . trade has met with a most prodigious shock.
>
> Times are very bad & precarious here & take my word, my good Friends, the times will be worse here, in short such is the situation of things here that we do not know who is and who not safe.

He wrote again on February 7: "Money is Extremely Scarce & trade very dull. If we are not reliev'd at home we must live upon our own produce & manufactures. We are terribly burthen'd, our Trade will decay." By early April his concern turned to the looming Stamp Act.

> I hear the stamp act is like to take place. It is very cruel, we were before much burthened, we shall not be able much longer to support trade, and in the end Great Britain must feel the ill effects of it. *I wonder the merchants and friends to America don't make some stir for us.*

Hancock wrote on September 30 that if it were to be "carry'd into Execution will entirely Stagnate Trade here, for it is universally determined here never to submit to it and the principal merchts here will by no means carry on Business under a Stamp." He wrote again on October 14.

> We are a people worth a saveing & our trade so much to your advantage worth keeping that it merits the notice of those on yr side who have the Conduct of it, but to *find nothing urg'd by the merchts on your side in our favour Really is extraordinary*. . . . I now tell you the whole Continent is so Rous'd that they will never suffer any one to Distribute the Stamps.

Hancock cannot "Carry on any Business" since "under this additional Burthen of the Stamp Act I cannot carry it on to any profit and we were before Cramp'd in our Trade & sufficiently Burthen'd, that any farther Taxes must Ruin us." A week later he raised the issue of rights.

> I will not be a slave. I have a Right to the Libertys & Privileges of the English Constitution, & I as an Englishman will enjoy them. We shall be in a most shocking situation after the 1st of November, & our state entire confusion, and nothing will reinstate us but the repeal of this act.[4]

On October 24, the *Pennsylvania Gazette* printed a letter from a Bristol (a trading town in England particularly important for commerce with the colonies) merchant, dated August, revealing the degree to which the British were feeling the effect of reduced trade with America.

> The present Situation of the Colonies alarms every Person who has any Connection with them. . . . The Avenues of Trade are all shut up. . . . We have no Remittances, and are at our Witts End for Want of Money to fulfill our Engagements with our Tradesmen.[5]

Nonimportation Associations

In late 1765, merchants at major ports in the colonies pledged to each other to not import British goods unless the Stamp Act was repealed. Such agreements were generally referred to as nonimportation associations and were primarily important as part of the politics of resistance—a threat—rather than as a further disruption of trade.[6]

New York took the first formal action. On October 31, merchants (more than two hundred of them) made resolutions about nonimportation.

> At a general meeting of the merchants of the city of New York, trading to Great Britain . . . to consider what was necessary to be done in the present situation of affairs with respect to the Stamp Act, and the melancholy state of the North American commerce, so greatly restricted by the impositions and duties

> established by the late acts of trade, they came to the following resolutions, viz.
>
> First. That in all orders they send out to Great Britain for goods or merchandise of any nature, kind, or quality whatsoever, usually imported from Great Britain, they will direct their correspondents not to ship them unless the Stamp Act be repealed.
>
> Secondly. That all orders already sent home, shall be countermanded by the very first conveyance; and the goods and merchandise thereby ordered, not to be sent unless upon the condition mentioned in the foregoing resolution.
>
> Thirdly. That no merchant will vend any goods or merchandise sent upon commission from Great Britain that shall be shipped from thence after the first day of January next unless upon the condition mentioned in the first resolution.

Prompted by the action of the merchants, the retailers made this agreement.

> We, the underwritten, retailers of goods, do hereby promise and oblige ourselves not to buy any goods, wares, or merchandises of any person or persons whatsoever that shall he shipped from Great Britain after the first day of January next unless the Stamp Act shall be repealed.[7]

General Gage wrote Conway on November 8.

> In order to gain the Merchants in Great Britain to their Interest, *the American Merchants have wrote that no dry goods may be sent out to them*, unless the Stamp Act is repealed, and some go as far as to say they will not pay their debts but upon that condition.

He understood the American rationale for the nonimportation: "They flatter themselves, from all these Circumstances, that the Parliament will be prevailed upon to repeal the act."[8]

On November 7, the merchants of Philadelphia established a non-importation association similar to that of New York.

> That the many difficulties they now labour under as a trading people are owing to the restrictions, prohibitions, and ill-advised regulations made in the several acts of the parliament of Great Britain, lately passed, to regulate the colonies; which have limited the exportation of some part of our country produce, increased the cost and expense of many articles of our importation, and cut off from us all means of supplying ourselves with specie enough even to pay the duties imposed on us, much less to serve as a medium of our trade.

The merchants then focus on the primary grievance.

> That the late unconstitutional law, the stamp-act, if carried into execution in this province, will further tend to prevent our making those remittances to Great Britain, for payment of old debts, or purchase of more goods.

They hope "that their example will stimulate the good people of this province to be frugal in their use and consumption of all [British] manufactures." The merchants also hope

> that their brethren, the merchants and manufacturers of Great Britain, will find their own interest so intimately connected with ours that they will be spurred on to befriend us from that motive.

After those statements of principle, the agreement calls for specific action.

> It is unanimously resolved and agreed that in all orders any of the subscribers to this [association] may send to Great Britain for goods, they shall and will direct their correspondents not to ship them until the stamp-act is repealed.[9]

Philadelphia merchants took further action to enlist support from their counterparts in Britain. Conservative Joseph Galloway, a wealthy landowner and future Loyalist, explained the strategy in a letter of November 29 to Franklin and Jackson.

> The Merchants of this City, greatly destrest with the present Circumstances of their Commerce, have transmitted to the Merchants and Manufacturers of Great Britain a Memorial Pointing out their Difficulties and hinting at the Remedies &c. which they Conceive will afford them the Desired Relief.
>
> They have been induced to take this Step, from an Expectation That the British Merchants and Manufacturers, who are deeply interested in our Trade . . . will Exert their Influence with the Parliament to remove the Cause of the Present Languishing State of American Commerce, so very detrimental to the Interest of Britain and Her Colonies.[10]

On December 9, Boston merchants drew up an agreement similar to those of New York and Philadelphia. John Hancock, later in December, had more to say to his agents.

> I will not import one single manufacture of Great Britain unless this grievous Burthen be removed, and I have further to pray the favor that if this act be not repealed, you make out and send me all my account & what ever Balance may be due to you I will endeavor to remit as soon as possible, as under the Burthen of the Stamp Act. I cannot carry on my business to any advantage & I cannot be a Slave to enrich Placemen.[11]

New York lieutenant governor Colden wrote Conway on December 13. Those opposed to the Stamp Act "have extended their views even to Great Britain in hopes of raising a spirit of Discontent among the Manufacturers there."

> They publish in the Newspapers that the Importation of British Manufactures are greatly decreased since the Duties on Amer-

> ican Trade, & that the Colonies are under a necessity of setting up the Manufactures which they otherwise would import from Great Britain.

Colden has considerable insight into the colonial strategy.

> The Merchants in New York, & some other Places have entered into an Agreement not to import any Goods from England the next year unless the Stamp act is Repealed. *This Scheme is calculated solely to influence the People in England.*[12]

AN EVENT THAT took place some two years later is not part of the Stamp Act story (having more to do with the aftermath of the Stamp Act crisis) but is nonetheless revealing as to the attitude of American merchants—or at least to the British perception of such an attitude—after the repeal of the Stamp Act. On March 21, 1768, Governor Bernard wrote the secretary of state regarding "meetings of the Merchants &c" during yet another conflict over customs duties on goods imported to the colonies. Referring to the meetings intended to lead to a nonimportation association, Bernard made the ominous statement that "this may be said to be the first movement of the Merchants against the Acts of parliament." Bernard understood the intent of the merchants.

> But it is scarce a Secret with any of them that the chief intent . . . is to *raise an alarm among the Merchants & Traders of Great Britain* & by means of popular discontent there to oblige the parliament to submit to their Terms in America. As this Game has been once before plaid with success [in 1765, during the Stamp Act crisis], it is no Wonder that they have great dependence upon it Now.

He could also see the ultimate goal.

In short, your Lordship may depend upon it that Nothing less than the abolition of all Acts imposing Duties is proposed. When that is done the transition to all other Acts of Parliament will be Very short & easy.[13]

Eight

Nullification

"The plan adopted by the populace was to force the Stamp Officers to a resignation & then to proceed in business as usual without the use of Stamps."

—Jared Ingersoll, November 1765

On November 1, 1765, the date scheduled for the Stamp Act to take effect, there were no stamp distributors and no stamps to be had. With a few minor exceptions, no stamped paper ever was used in the manner intended by the act. Actions taken by the Americans—intimidation of and violent acts against stamp distributors, customs officers, and other British officials—nullified the act.

The process began in mid-1765 and proceeded in parallel with resolutions, petitions, and nonimportation. The first mob actions took place in August, leading to the destruction of property and the coerced resignation of stamp distributors. By late in the year the rise of informal but well-organized militant patriot organizations made it clear that any attempt to enforce the act would require significant British military might—more than those forces retained in the colonies following the Seven Years' War.

Boston Shows the Way

The story begins with the effect of the Virginia Resolves. On July 20, Governor Bernard wrote John Pownall, a personal friend as well as secretary to the Board of Trade, that after a period of calm "there came hither in a Rhode Island Newspaper [the last week in June] an Account of some resolutions of the House of burgesses of Virginia." The resolutions raised "the Spirit of Rebellion . . . [and] roused up the Boston Politicians."[1] The "Politicians" in turn, roused up a mob on August 14, leading to Boston setting an example for active resistance.

Governor Bernard tells a vivid story of the mobbish activity, writing the Board of Trade on August 15.

> I am extremely concerned that I am obliged to give your Lordships the Relation that is to follow; as it will reflect disgrace upon this Province, and bring the Town of Boston under great difficulties. Two or three months ago, I thought that this People would have submitted to the Stamp Act without actual Opposition. Murmurs indeed were continually heard, but they seemed to be such as would in time die away; But the publishing of the Virginia Resolves proved an Alarm bell to the disaffected.

He describes the action of August 14, seeing what at first seems simply to be rowdy behavior.

> Yesterday Morning at break of day was discovered hanging upon a Tree in a Street of the Town an Effigy with inscriptions shewing that it was intended to represent Mr. Oliver, the Secretary, who had lately accepted the Office of Stamp Distributor. Some of the Neighbours offered to take it down, but they were given to know that would not be permitted. Many Gentlemen, especially some of the Council, treated it as a boyish sport that did not deserve the Notice of the Governor & Council.

(Such display of an effigy was often a signal for impending action, even violence against the person represented.) A mob soon formed and once darkness fell moved to the prospective "Stamp Office, & pulled it down to the Ground in five minutes."

> From thence they went to Mr. Olivers House, before which they beheaded the Effigy, & broke all the Windows next to the Street; then they carried the Effigy to Fort hill near Mr. Olivers House, where they burnt the Effigy in a Bonfire made of the Timber they had pulled down from the Building. [The mob then] beat in all the doors & windows of the Garden front, & entered the House.
>
> As soon as they had got possession, they searched about for Mr. Oliver, declaring they would kill him. [Eventually] they were diverted from this Pursuit by a Gentleman telling them that Mr. Oliver was gone with the Governor to the Castle [Castle William, a British fort on an island in Boston harbor]: Otherwise he would certainly have been murdered.

The militia was unable to control the situation.

> I should have mentioned before that I sent a written order to the Colonel of the Regiment of Militia to beat an Alarm; he answered that it would signify nothing, for as soon as the drum was heard, the drummer would be knocked down, and the drum broke; he added that probably all the drummers of the Regiment were in the Mob.

Bernard continues the letter on August 16.

> In the afternoon of Yesterday, Sevral Gentlemen applied to Mr. Oliver, to advise him to make a publick declaration, that he would resign the Office, & never act in it; without which they said, his House would be immediately destroyed, & his Life in continual Danger. Upon which he was obliged to authorise some Gentlemen to declare in public, that he would immediately apply for leave to resign, & would not act in the Office.

He describes the mob.

> Every one agrees that this riot has exceeded all others known here, both in the Vehemence of Action & mischievousness of intention: & never had any Mob so many abettors of Consequence as this is supposed to have had. It is said there were 50 Gentlemen Actors in this Scene disguised with trousers & Jackets on [such apparel being indicative of low social class], besides a much larger Number behind the Curtain.

He discusses the participation of gentlemen.

> It is said also, that these disguised Gentlemen proceeded no farther than the burning the Effigy, & then departed, & had no hand in storming the House: & it is certain that many Gentlemen, who approved of hanging & burning the Effigy, took the Pains the next day to prevent any further Mischief being done to Mr. Oliver or his House.

Bernard describes the overall temper of the town.

> The common talk of the Town is that the Stamp Act shall not be executed here; that a Man who offers a stamped Paper to sell will be immediately killed; that all the power of Great Britain shall not oblige them to submit to the Stamp Act; that they will die upon the Place first, &c, &c. . . . In truth, it will be impossible to attempt to carry the Act into execution, untill fresh Orders & Powers shall come from England.[2]

Bernard later explains that on August 15 "Mr. Oliver was obliged to treat with the heads of the mob (who, they say, are some of the principal Men of the Town) for the ransom of his house & the Safety of his Life, which could be obtained by no other Means than by his engaging to resign the Stamp Office & never to act in it."[3]

How did such a mob arise and come to be under the direction of the principal men of the town? In separate letters, Bernard and

Hutchinson tell the story. First of all, the mechanism for taking action was ready at hand. In Boston, "for a long time past it has been Customary for two parties in this Town denominated from the North & South End to fight with one another on the 5 of November with the Image of a Pope at the head of each party." (November 5, Pope's Day, was commemoration of a seventeenth-century event in England more widely known as Guy Fawkes Day.)

But the riot of August 14–15 was not such roughhouse; it was instigated by a secretive group of radical patriots who realized—given Parliament's rejection (the previous February) of the petitions of 1764 from colonial legislatures—that words alone would not serve to prevent the Stamp Act from coming into effect. The core group of radicals called themselves the Loyal Nine—a group of "middling" men such as artisans, printers, masons, carpenters, and shopkeepers. (The Loyal Nine became the founding element of the Boston Sons of Liberty, a patriotic organization that in the next few months would rise up in every colony in opposition to the Stamp Act.) They saw that if stamped paper were to be destroyed, or if there were no distributors to sell the stamped paper, the act would be nullified. The colonists would be justified it was thought—no violation of the law—that they could go on with business as usual.

The Loyal Nine engaged the services of the leaders of the south and north end forces to direct their violence against the hated Stamp Act. Bernard explains.

> The Captain of the South End, Mr. Mackintosh a Shoemaker, was notoriously the leader of that Mob, which was raised in the South end, & acted Visibly under the directions of Persons much his Superiors. . . . Two Gentlemen, called the richest Merchants in this Town, entertained the principal Men of these parties, & reconciled them to one another, for other Purposes, I fear, than burning a Pope. [The Loyal Nine and the two mob leaders planned for united action in the days before the riot of August 14.][4]

Lieutenant Governor Hutchinson explained that the mob consisted of

> the rabble of the town of Boston headed by one Mackintosh. . . . When there is occasion to burn or hang effigies or pull down houses these are employed, but . . . they are some what controuled by a superior set consisting of the master masons, carpenters, &c of the town.

"When any thing of more importance is to be determined as opening the custom house or any matters of trade these are under the direction of a committee of merchants."[5]

Governor Bernard had all along believed—as his private sentiments shared with officials in London—that before taxation such as the Stamp Act could be attempted, the colonies must be reorganized along the lines he had proposed in his *Principles of Law and Polity.* On August 18, he wrote John Pownall: "To introduce parliamentary Taxations into America before the establishment of a power sufficient to enforce obedience to them is in my opinion beginning at the wrong End. The People know that at present they may chuse whether they will submit to be taxed or not." He emphasized "how weak & impotent the Authority of American Governors is in regard to popular tumults."[6]

On August 22, Bernard again wrote the Board of Trade: "I come now to pursue the subject of my letter to your Lordships dated the 15 & 16." He tells a woeful tale.

> For my own part, I am suffered to remain unmolested as yet, & am allowed to be the Governor in the Council Chamber, provided I dont attempt it anywhere else. But in my present defenceless State, I consider myself only as a Prisoner at large, being wholly in the power of the People. . . . I am wholly without Authority.

He goes on to analyze the mood of the people.

> It is difficult to conceive the fury which at present possesses the People of Boston of all Orders & degrees of Men. If a Gentleman in common Conversation signifies his disapprobation of

> this insurrection, his Person is immediately in Danger. A Gentleman having said that notwithstanding what had passed, he would accept of the Stamp Office [i.e., to replace Oliver], a day was fixed for pulling down his House, & it was prevented not without difficulty.[7]

On August 31, Bernard wrote to the secretary of state that the mobbish behavior has "been carried to much greater lengths than what I have before informed Your Lordship of." He describes a riot of August 26 resulting in the destruction of the homes of British officials. The mob went to the home of an official of the admiralty, William Story, then "broke into it & tore it all to pieces; & took out all the books & papers among which were all the records of the Court of Admiralty & carried them to the bonfire & there burnt them. . . . From thence they went to Mr. Hallowell's, Comptroller of the Customs, broke into his house & destroyed & carried off evry thing of Value, with about 30 pounds sterling in cash." Bernard goes on that "the grand Mischief of all was to come."

> The Lieut Governor had been apprized that there was an evil Spirit gone forth against him: but being conscious that he had not in the least deserved to be made a party in regard to the stamp Act or the Customhouse, he rested in full Security that the Mob would not attack him; & he sat Supper with his family when he received advice that the Mob were coming to him. He immediately sent away his children & determined to stay in the house himself.

Fortunately, he was convinced to leave the house, "which was undoubtedly the Occasion of saving his Life."

> For as soon as The Mob had got into the house with a most irresistible fury they immediately lookt about for him to murder him. . . . They went to work with a rage scarce to be exemplified by the most Savage people. Evry thing moveable was destroyed in the most minute manner, except such things of Value as were

worth carrying off, among which was near 1000 pounds sterling in Specie, besides a great quantity of family plate &c.

The violence "was now becoming a War of plunder, of general levelling & taking away the distinction of rich & poor: so that those Gentlemen who had promoted & approved the cruel treatment of Mr. Oliver, became now as fearful for themselves as the most loyal person in the Town could be. . . . Great pains are taken to separate the two riots; what was done against Mr. Oliver is still approved of, as a necessary Declaration of their resolution not to submit to the stamp Act."[8]

Bernard wrote General Gage the next day.

> I doubt not but you will have an account of the riots at Boston, upon the business of the Stamp Act before this comes to hand. The Mob was so general & so supported, that all civil power ceased in an instant, & I had not the least authority to oppose or quiet the mob. You are sensible how extreamly weak an American Governor is in regard to popular tumults, without a file of Men at his Command, & having no regular troops, at present, within call.

He almost, but not quite, asks for military support.

> More mischief is daily expected: Where it will end no body knows. In short, The Town of Boston is in the Possession of an incensed & implacable Mob . . . I have nothing to do, but to apply to you, as his Majesty's Military Commander in chief; & I can only recommend to you to use such means as you shall think proper to preserve his Majestys Dominion over this Town.[9]

Gage, however, was constitutionally barred from using troops without an explicit request from the civil authority.

On September 28, Bernard wrote to Secretary of State Conway to report the latest situation in Boston. He states in his letter "that the

Violences of the mob had intimidated some of the best people in the province." He also makes the desperate report that "if things dont take another turn before the first of November the appearance of Government will cease; as the real Authority has ever since the first riot."[10]

On October 26, Bernard wrote to John Pownall that the Massachusetts assembly intended "to provide for keeping open the public Offices without the use of Stamps." But a few days later he wrote that since "it would have been admitting that they would use them if they could get them," the assembly decided against such action. "So the thing, I believe, is dropt."[11]

Bernard wrote Pownall again on November 1. The previous afternoon, the commanding officer of the guard

> said he could not get a Drummer to beat a Drum; one who had attempted it had his Drum broke; the others were bought off; the People would not muster; &c. . . . [However,] we were assured that if the Guard was dismissed the Town would be quiet, otherwise not; that there would be a procession the next day, but there should be nothing in it to affront this Government.

He turns to events of that day: "There is an high Tree standing in the Town . . . which is called the *Tree of Liberty*: It has a Copper plate fixed upon it, giving it that title in a pompous inscription dated Augt 14, 1765, the day that Mr. Olivers House was demolished" (the tree became a popular gathering place for Stamp Act protests). "On this Tree early in the Morning of Novr. 1st (which was ushered in by the tolling of bells) were found hanging [taunting effigies]." Bernard had expected violence on the planned effective date of the Stamp Act, but there was no violence, only orderly events of marching and demonstrating. The leaders of events in Boston had engaged McIntosh to keep order and discipline, not to lead a riot. The letter continues on November 5 with an indication of colonial disdain for the requirements of the act: "You must know that the News Papers come out unstamped as regularly as they did before the 1st of November."

Bernard notes that "this Government is entirely subverted." He dramatizes the thought with a woebegone postscript on November 8: "There is such an appearance of tranquillity that I may remain here a Cypher some time longer."[12]

On November 23, Bernard wrote to Secretary at War Barrington with reflections on the resistance: "A little Consideration would have made it at least doubtfull whether an inland Taxation of the Americans was practicable or equitable at that Time."

> It must have been supposed that such an Innovation as a Parliamentary Taxation would cause a great Alarm & meet with much Opposition in most parts of America; It was quite new to the people & had no visible Bounds set to it; The Americans declared that they would not submit to it before the Act passed; & there was the greatest probability that it would require the utmost Power of Government to carry it into Execution.

However, the problem was larger than the Stamp Act.

> The Question will not be whether there shall be a Stamp Act or not; but whether America *shall or shall not be Subject to the Legislature* of Great Britain.

In a particularly direct and expressive manner, Bernard makes the case for "shall":

> The Right of the Parliament of Great Britain to make Laws for the American Colonies is founded upon its being the *Supreme Imperial Legislature*, to which all Members of the Empire, whether represented or not, are subject in all Matters & Things & in Manner & Form as shall be judged most convenient for the whole.[13]

On November 30, Bernard complained to the Board of Trade about the "ungovernable state" of Boston, stating that "immense pains have been taken to poison the Minds of the people" by the

"Newspapers which have been published here for 4 months past." In consequence,

> In this town all the Power is in the hands of the people, out of which, under pretence of uniting two parties in the town, are formed two companies under two protest Captains who are said to be able to muster 400 men on a short warning. Two or three Gentlemen of fortune profess to have the Command of these bands; and it is hoped they have; as the Governor & evry other Officer of the Crown lie at their Mercy.[14]

In December, Bernard received two letters from London purporting to give guidance regarding stamp distributors. His response provides a striking image of the situation in Massachusetts late in the year. First, the two letters from London.

On September 14, the Treasury, receiving upsetting news from the colonies about the Virginia Resolves, gave additional orders to colonial governors, sent by secretary to the treasury Charles Lowndes.

> I am directed by the Lords Commissioners of His Majesty's Treasury to Signify to your Excellency their desire that you will give your aid and assistance to the Distributor of Stamps within your Government.[15]

On October 8, Grey Cooper (another secretary to the treasury), prompted by receipt in London of Bernard's first reports about rioting in Boston, sent him firm direction.

> The Lords Commissioners . . . are pleased to direct your Excellency to see that the Stamps be duly distributed until a Distributor be appointed by My Lords . . . [and to] enforce a due Obedience to the Laws, and to take care that His Majesty's Revenue Suffers no Detriment or Diminution.[16]

Bernard responded to Cooper on December 22: "I have this day received a letter from Mr Lowndes dated Sepr 14, & a letter from you dated Octr 8."

> In the latter, you signify to me that the Lords Commissioners of the Treasury direct me to see that the Stamps be duly distributed untill a Distributor be appointed. I doubt not but long before this letter will come to your hands, their Lordships will be apprised how impossible it is for me to obey their Commands.
>
> At this time I have no real Authority in this place, & am so much in the hands of the People, that if it was to be known here that I had received a power to distribute the Stamps, I should have my House surrounded & be obliged, at least, to give public Assurance that I would not undertake the Business.

He also comments on the lack of authoritative information from London: "Altho' I never received any orders concerning the Stamp Act (untill this day) nor even a Copy of the Act, I thought it my duty to do all I could to get it carried into execution."[17]

More Riots and Threats

Following the August mob violence in Boston, additional riots soon followed, the most noteworthy being in Newport, Rhode Island, and in New York City.

Newport

On August 27–28, a mob scene similar to that in Boston developed in Newport. Rather than analyze the rioting—more mobs, effigies, burning, destruction, and a successful demand for the stamp distributor (Augustus Johnson) to resign his commission on August 29—it is more revealing to describe the resulting disruption of trade.[18]

This letter of August 30 is addressed to the "Governor and Company of Rhode Island" from John Robinson, Collector (of the port of Newport) and two other officers of the customs. The letter was sent from the man-of-war HMS *Cygnet* resting in Newport harbor.

> What has happened yesterday and the night before, and the threats denounced in that time, and to this moment, to our persons and property . . . has determined us to shut up His

> Majesty's custom house, till the government affords us such protection and support, as will enable us to attend to our duties with safety . . . we cannot open the custom house till you, gentlemen, [provide] assistance; and we desire to know what protection and support you will give us.

The next day, Governor Samuel Ward brashly claimed that he "can give you the most absolute assurance that every thing is perfectly tranquil, and that you may immediately return to town with all the safety imaginable." Robinson did not believe him, continuing to shutter the customs house (stopping all seaborne commerce in Newport) until September 2 when the governor relented and provided a guard force.[19]

The circular letter of September 14 from the Treasury reached Newport in late December. Governor Ward's December 26 response to the letter gives additional insight into the situation late in the year.

> On the 21st instant, I received a letter, dated 14th September last, from Mr. Lowndes, signifying to me Your Lordships' desire that I would give the distributor of the stamped papers in this colony my aid and assistance in whatever may relate to his duty in the execution of his office, &c.

It turns out that "aid and assistance" has been overtaken by events since the chief distributor "hath resigned that office."

> People of every rank and condition are so unanimous in their opinion that the operation of the act for levying stamp duties in America would be inconsistent with their natural and just rights and privileges, injurious to His Majesty's service and the interest of Great Britain, and incompatible with the very being of this colony, that no person, I imagine, will undertake to execute that office.

Ward goes on to predict "the operation of the stamp act would be swift and inevitable ruin to the government." However, if the "ancient rights and liberties" were restored, everything would return to normal.[20]

New York

Lieutenant Governor Colden received this resignation letter from distributor James McEvers on August 30.

> Since the late riott at Boston & the inflammatory papers lately printed in the Colonies, People of this City are so incensed against me, as a distributor of Stamps for this Province, that I find it will be attended with the greatest risque of my Person and Fortune to attempt, and indeed impossible for me to execute, the Office.[21]

The next day, in a casual letter to a friend, Colden characterized McEvers as being "terrified by the suffering & ill usage the Stamp officer met with at Boston, & the threats he has received at New York." Colden remained optimistic: "Notwithstanding of this I hope with the assistance I expect to defeat all their Measures & that the Stamps shall be delivered in proper time after their arrival. I shall not be intimidated."[22]

Colden wrote General Gage on September 2.

> The only method in my opinion to prevent mischief is to have such a Military force present as may effectually discourage all opposition to the Laws. A weak force which the Seditious can have any hopes of overcoming may be productive of great mischiefs.[23]

Colden showed that he shared a concern with Governor Bernard, writing Secretary of State Conway on September 23.

> Soon after it was known that Stamp Duties were by Act of Parliament to be paid in the Colonies, virulent papers were published in the Weekly Newspapers, filled with every falsehood that malice could invent to serve their purpose of exciting the

> people to disobedience of the Laws and to Sedition. At first they only denied the authority of Parliament to lay internal taxes in the Colonies but at last they have denyed the Legislative Authority of the Parliament in the Colonies, and these papers continue to be published.

He sees a deeper purpose: "It is evident that a secret Correspondence has been carryed on throughout all the Colonies; & that it has been concerted to deter by violence the Distributors of Stamps from Executing their office, and to destroy the stamped Paper when it arrives."[24]

General Gage also wrote to Conway on September 23: "The Resolves of the Assembly of Virginia, which you will have seen, gave the Signal for a general outcry over the Continent . . . they have been applauded as the Protectors and Assertors of American Liberty."

> The general Scheme, concerted throughout seems to have been, first, by Menace or Force, to oblige the Stamp Officers to resign their Employments, in which they have generally succeeded; and next, to destroy the Stampt Papers upon their Arrival; that having no Stamps, Necessity might be an Escape for the Dispatch of Business without them; and that, before they could be replaced, the Clamor and outcry of the People, with Addresses and Remonstrances from the Assemblys, might procure a Repeal of the Act.

He discusses the violence in Boston and Newport and notes that "the Neighbouring Provinces seem inclined to follow these Examples, but were prevented by the almost general Resignation of the Stamp Officers." He demonstrates unwarranted optimism that everything "is quiet at present and a calm seems to have succeeded the Storm. People talk and Reason more cooly and begin to perceive that Trade and all Business whatsoever will be thrown into great Difficultys without the Stamps." However, he admits the storm has not yet fully passed. "Papers are daily expected, and the Act to take Place on the first of November, the final Issue of this Affair will be soon determined."[25]

Stamps arrived at New York on October 23. John Montresor, a British military engineer working on a survey of New York, described events in his journal.

> 23rd. Arrived the vessel with the Stamps . . . 2000 people (mob) on the Battery expecting the Stamps would be landed, but were disappointed. However they were secretly landed in the night and deposited in the Fort [Fort George, in upper Manhattan] and took charge of by the Governor.[26]

The arrival of stamps prompted this handbill to be posted around town on October 24:

> Pro Patria
> The first Man that Either distributes or makes use of Stampt Paper, let him take care of his House, Person & Effects.
> VOX POPULI
> We dare[27]

The planned date of implementation saw dramatic mob violence in New York. Colden wrote to Conway on November 5.

> On the evening of the first day of this month the Mob began to collect together, & after it became dark, they came up to the Fort Gate with a great number of boys carrying Torches & a scaffold on which two Immages were placed: One to represent the Governor in his grey hairs, & the other the Devil by his side.

In town, the mob burnt "my Chariot, a single Horse chair & two sledges. . . . A great number of gentlemen of the Town if they can be call'd so, stood around to observe the outrage on their King's Governor." At the same time, the garrison of the fort was "on the Ramparts with Preparation sufficient to have destroyed [the mob], but not a single return was made in words or otherwise from any Man in the Fort while this egregious Insult was performing." Although Colden characterized troops in the fort, commanded by Major

Thomas James, as being commendably stoic, part of their reluctance to start a conflict was that they were badly outnumbered by the mob—a hundred or so troops to more than two thousand irate New Yorkers. Colden said that the mob also destroyed the house of Major James "at the same time threatening to take away his life in the most shameful manner."[28] Colden directed James to personally carry the letter to London and report to Conway.

General Gage wrote to Conway on November 4.

> It is difficult to say, from the highest to the lowest, who has not been accessory to this insurrection, either by writing or mutual agreements to oppose the act, by what they are pleased to term all legal opposition to it. . . . This affair stands in all the provinces, that unless the act, from its own nature, enforce itself, *nothing but a very considerable military force can do it.*[29]

Gage, in his letter of November 8 (first mentioned in chapter 7) provided more insight into the American strategy: "Their first plan of Clamor, in terrifying the Stamp Officers, and even threats of Rebellion to prevent the Stamps being issued, has been compleated throughout."[30]

Gage wrote to Conway on December 21, reaffirming that the violence was directed by men of substance.

> The Plan of the People of Property has been to raise the lower Class to prevent the Execution of the Law, and as far as Riots and Tumults went against Stamp-Masters and other Obstructions to the Issuing of the Stamps, they encouraged, and many perhaps joined them.

Mob violence was intended to influence British public opinion.

> They have wrote many Letters to their Correspondents in England, in which they throw the Blame upon the unruly Populace, Magnifying the Force and determined Resolution of the People to oppose the Execution of the Law by every Means, with the

> View to terrify and frighten the People of England into a Repeal of the Act.

And to influence British merchants.

> And the Merchants having Countermanded the Goods they had Wrote for unless it was repealed, they make no Doubt that many Trading Towns and principal Merchants in London will assist them to accomplish their Ends.

There is planning behind the riots.

> The Lawyers are the Source from whence the Clamors have flowed in every Province. In this Province Nothing Publick is transacted without them, and it is to be wished that even the Bench was free from Blame.
>
> The whole Body of Merchants in general; Assembly Men, Magistrates, &c. have been united in this Plan of Riots, and without the Influence and Instigation of these, the inferior People would have been quiet. Very great Pains was taken to rouse them before they Stirred. The Sailors who are the only People who may be properly Stiled Mob, are entirely at the Command of the Merchants who employ them.[31]

Sons of Liberty

Patriots in every colony banded together to oppose the Stamp Act with threats and intimidation directed toward stamp distributors and other British officials, often ending with actual violence. By late 1765, such organizations began to adopt the nom de guerre "Sons of Liberty," the phrase used by Isaac Barre in the House of Commons during debate on passage of the Stamp Act. Radical, militant, nominally secret, and working toward intercolonial cooperation, the Sons of Liberty, although differing from colony to colony, largely took their membership from the middling and upper levels of society. For action however—forcing government to bend to the will of the radical leaders—they relied upon men of little property or rank, wage earners such as shop assistants and sailors. The organization arose earliest and most belligerently in New York and Connecticut. New York was the location of the bulk of the British forces and was expected to be the starting point for any British enforcement of the Stamp Act through the use of armed force.[32]

The riot in New York on November 1 "convinced the gentlemen who were standing up for the rights of the colonies that it was necessary to have leaders to manage the mob." They met on November 6 "and it was proposed, that a committee be appointed. . . . They agreed among themselves to sign all the letters with their several names, and to open a correspondence with all the colonies." The committee became active and was the foundation for "another set of corresponding sons of liberty . . . to strengthen the opposition of the colonies to parliamentary taxation."[33]

Later in November Alexander Colden (son of Lieutenant Governor Colden) described what was going on.

> The Sons of Liberty of this place have wrote to Phila. that if they do not make [their stamp distributor] resign as fully as the other Distributors have done, they will disown them & hold no longer Correspondence with them.[34]

A plan to deal with the coming conflict was established by resolutions made in New London, Connecticut, on December 10.

> At a meeting of a large assembly of the respectable populace in New London the 10th of December 1765, the following resolves were unanimously come into.
> 1st. That every form of government rightfully founded, originates from the consent of the people.
> 2d. That the boundaries set by the people in all constitutions are the only limits within which any officer can lawfully exercise authority.
> 3d. That whenever those bounds are exceeded, the people have a right to reassume the exercise of that authority which by nature they had before they delegated it to individuals.

Further resolutions state the illegitimacy of the Stamp Act and "that it is the duty of every person in the colonies to oppose by every lawful means the execution of those acts imposed on them . . . and in order effectually to prevent the execution" of the act, the resolves reject all advocacy of passive behavior.

> It is presumed no person will publicly, in the pulpit or otherwise, inculcate the doctrine of passive obedience, or any other doctrine tending to quiet the minds of the people, in a tame submission to any unjust impositions.[35]

Governor Bernard reported to Conway on January 19, 1766, about a recent agreement to oppose any British attempt to enforce the Stamp Act by force of arms.

> I have made diligent enquiry into the truth of a report that the People of New York had sent Agents to Connecticut & Boston to concert what Number of Men might be depended upon to assist in opposing the Kings Forces entring New York.

Bernard enclosed a description of events "from the Mouth of a Gentleman, who was present at the time & place." The meeting took place in a tavern in New London. "It was expected Troops would be sent from England to enforce their Submission to the Stamp Act; that it was necessary for them to unite in opposition to the English Forces upon this occasion; that most probably New York would be attacked first, & therefore Connecticut ought to march in defence of New York."[36]

The meeting referred to by Bernard had taken place on December 25 between the Sons of Liberty of New York and Connecticut; it established, "Certain reciprocal and mutual agreements, concessions and associations." They vowed allegiance to the king, and asserted that they were not revolutionary, but wished to restore the past and preserve the British constitution, "not in the least desiring any alteration or innovation in the grand bulwark of their liberties." But if necessary,

> they do reciprocally resolve and determine to march with the utmost dispatch . . . to the relief those that shall, are, or may be in danger from the stamp-act, or its promoters and abettors.

The final section of the agreement states the intent to create an intercolonial movement.

> And finally, that they will, to the utmost of their power, endeavour to bring about, accomplish, and perfect the like association with all the colonies on the continent for the like salutary purposes and no other.[37]

Resignation of the Stamp Distributors

On the planned date for implantation of the Stamp Act there were no stamp distributors. In every colony they were forced to resign by violence or the threat of violence. Those for Massachusetts, Rhode Island, and New York were ousted in August. On September 3, New Jersey stamp distributor William Coxe resigned his office. Governor William Franklin was surprised, expressing belief that the act would be peaceably executed.

> I have as yet received no directions from the Ministry relative to the Stamp Act, but if I should be impowered to appoint an Officer, pro Tempore . . . I doubt not but I shall be able to procure one that will execute the Office, with little or no Trouble.[38]

The New Hampshire distributor, George Meserve (who had been visiting England), arrived in Boston on September 8, the ship later bound for Portsmouth. A Boston mob would not allow the ship to dock until September 10. Meserve wisely resigned his commission before going ashore and was then welcomed by the crowd.[39]

John Hughes, appointed for Pennsylvania and Delaware, wrote on September 8 to Benjamin Franklin.

> You are now from Letter to Letter to suppose each may be the

> last that you will receive from your old Friend, as the Spirit or Flame of Rebellion is got to a high Pitch amongst the North Americans; and it seems to me that a Sort of Frenzy or Madness has got such hold of the People of all Ranks, that I fancy some Lives will be lost before this Fire is put out.[40]

Later in September Hughes was threatened with violence if he did not resign. Demands reached a crescendo on October 5 when the stamps arrived in Philadelphia. He finally wrote Lieutenant Governor John Penn on October 8 that the ringleaders of the disturbance "declared and vowed destruction to my person and property if I refused to gratify them in their demands. My resignation is accordingly made."[41]

On September 19, Connecticut stamp distributor Jared Ingersoll was seized by a body of troops (over five hundred men on horseback) and forced to resign. As part of his resignation he made the point "that I believed I was as averse to the Stamp-Act as any of them; that I had accepted my Appointment to this Office, I thought upon the fairest Motives." On November 2, he wrote a lengthy explanation to the stamp commissioners in London, including this overview: "The plan adopted by the populace was to force the Stamp Officers to a resignation & then to proceed in business as usual without the use of Stamps."[42]

The Maryland stamp distributor, Zacharia Hood, wrote Benjamin Franklin on September 23 (dated at New York). He reported that Maryland was "extreamly heated," and that a mob "pull'd down my House and obliged me to flie." His flight was as good as a resignation. Then, on November 28, he was forced to resign by the Sons of Liberty of New York.[43]

When the appointed Virginia stamp distributor, George Mercer, returned on October 30 from a visit to England, he was met by a large crowd. In a letter to the Board of Trade on November 3, Lieutenant Governor Fauquier described the event, showing that the Virginia gentlemen were not remaining "behind the curtain" as in other colonies.

> This Concourse of people I should call a Mob, did I not know that it was chiefly if not altogether composed of Gentlemen of property in the Colony . . . [They] demanded of him an Answer whether he would resign or act in his Office as Distributor of the Stamps.

Continued threats forced Mercer's resignation on October 31, the day before the Stamp Act was to take effect. Fauquier refused the resignation, writing the Board of Trade that "I did not think myself authorized to accept it. . . . If I accepted the Resignation, I must appoint another, and I was well convinced I could not find one to accept of it." Fauquier wrote Conway on November 5, stating "the Dissatisfaction of the people of this Colony against receiving the Stamps is too strong for my poor Abilities to overcome. The Flame is spread thro' all the Continent, and one Colony supports another in their Disobedience to superior powers."[44]

South Carolina lieutenant governor William Bull wrote the Board of Trade on November 3: "Upon the arrival of the stamp papers on the 20th ultimo a great concourse of men assembled," causing Bull to secure the stamped paper under military guard. But the crowd of two thousand men turned angry: "Their fury was then directed towards striking a terror into the stamp officers if they persisted to perform their duty." Ultimately, the mob was successful in pressuring stamp distributor Caleb Lloyd to offer his resignation on October 28; he "consented to decline acting until the sense of the Parliament of Great Britain should be known upon the joint petition of the colonies which is now on the anvil at New York."

> Although these very numerous assemblies of the people bore the appearance of common populace, yet there is great reason to apprehend they were animated and encouraged by some considerable men who stood behind the curtain.[45]

The original appointee for North Carolina declined the office, leaving no distributor on November 1. Dr. William Houston, appointed by a letter from London that reached him on November 16, immediately resigned as demanded "by several hundred people in semi-military array, with drums beating and flags flying."[46]

Georgia was a modest exception to the rule of nullification. Although there was no stamp distributor or stamps available on November 1, when distributor George Angus arrived on January 3, stamps were briefly available and sold, but only for the purpose of allowing shipping to move. Alert to the antagonism of the colonists, Agnus did not resign, but in effect a resignation, simply disappeared from the province at the end of January.[47]

Business Paused then Resumed

In the absence of stamps, government officials in the colonies needed to decide what to do about normal business, the most urgent being ports—clearance of ships and cargo—and courts of law. The lack of stamped paper at first led to considerable disruption of colonial business in most colonies, British officials at first refusing to open civil courts or to clear ships into or out of ports.

The Sons of Liberty played an important role in forcing business as usual, concerned that any disruption might be construed as a form of acknowledgment that the Stamp Act was binding on the colonies. Their success was mixed in 1765, but largely successful by the early months of 1766.[48]

Joseph Galloway wrote Franklin in late November that stamped papers had arrived in Philadelphia "but the Mob will not suffer them to be used, and the Public Officers of Justice and of Trade, being under Obligation of their Oaths and liable to the Penalties of the Statute, will not proceed in their Duties without them." No British official would clear ships and if they did so without stamped papers, "Men of War threaten to Seize them as forfeited for want of Papers agreeable to the Laws of trade. . . . I can see no relief but from an immediate repeal of the Act."[49]

Stamp distributor Andrew Oliver was forced to again resign, publicly, on December 17. Bernard wrote Conway the next day that "there was not the least pretence for this insult."

> It was designed as an Insult upon the Kings Authority; as a Terror to the Kings Officers; and to show them that they were

> nothing in the Eyes or the Hands of the People. I myself must expect to be called to the Tree of Liberty if I stay much longer in this Town.[50]

Surveyor General Temple was quickly convinced. The December 23 *Boston Evening-Post* had this announcement, a clear indication of moving toward business as usual.

> The Custom-House in this Town is now opened for the Clearing out of Vessels, a Certificate being given, That no Stamp-Papers are to be had.[51]

Governor Bernard was near the end of his rope. On December 19 he wrote Conway, pleading "that all real power in this Town is in the hands of the People."

> Power devolves to the people; that where there is no other redress, as in the Stamp Act, the people should resume their power: therefore they recommend, with threats against disobedience, that the public officers should proceed in their business without stamps. This is a formal Resumption of Government by the people.

At the end, he sends Conway the expectations of those with the real power.

> I think it proper to add to my foregoing conjecture the following instance, being the copy of a paper stuck up in the Town house under the Council chamber.
>
> Open your Courts,
> and let Justice prevail:
> Open your Offices,
> and let not Trade fail.
> For if those Men in power will not act,
> We'll get some that will, is Actual Fact.[52]

Bernard wrote the Board of Trade on January 18, 1766: The popular leaders, via town meetings, were forcing business to resume without stamps, "threatning Great Britain with a defection, to oblige her to submit to their own terms, both in repealing the Stamp Act, & letting the Government proceed according to such ideas of policy & civil rights as they in their present plenitude of power have formed to themselves."

> The plan is to make all the people of the province equally delinquent with themselves by obliging all public officers to transact business without stamps & thereby make the rejection of the stamp Act which otherwise would be very partial & local, general & universal.
>
> They first began with the Customhouse officers, who after an altercation of 3 weeks, submitted to do their business without stamps; but not 'till it was known that the [mob] had fixed upon a day for a rising.[53]

Bernard wrote Conway a series of letters that summed up the situation in early 1766. On January 21 he wrote that "the Town of Boston has by intimidation obliged the Judges & Officers . . . to do their business without stamps; they have instructed their Members to use their utmost endeavours that justice be administred in a ma[n]ner contrary to Act of parliament throughout the province." On January 25 he wrote that the assembly was encouraging the courts to open "in defiance of the Act of parliament." He added that expectations of the radical faction in the assembly "have been a good deal encouraged by letters from some Merchants in London; one of which, who claims an intimacy with a Minister of State, says in positive terms, that it is resolved to take off the stamp duty. These advices tho much contradicted by others, tend greatly to counterwork any attempts to procure a submission to the act." And on February 28 he wrote again: hard truths about the colonial resistance.

> The Stamp Act is become in itself a matter of Indifference; it is swallowed up in the Importance of the Effects of which it has

been the Cause. The taxing the Americans by the Parliament *has brought their very Subjection to the Crown of Great Britain in Question.*

And as the Relation between Great Britain & the Colonies has not only been never settled, but scarce ever formally canvassed, It is the less surprizing, that the Ideas of it on one Side of the Water & on the other are so widely different. To reconcile these, & to ascertain the nature of the Subjection of the Colonies to the Crown of Great Britain, will be a work of Time & difficulty; even tho' the Stamp Act should be removed to pave the Way for It.[54]

PART THREE

Retreat

"If we do not repeal it, the disorder in America [and] the distress of our manufactures at home [will continue]. If we do repeal it, no minister will venture to tax them again. The Americans will never submit when they see resistance is the best argument for relief, and you will have the same argument urged not against this law alone but against every other which they do not perfectly approve of."

—Charles Jenkinson, February 1766

Nine

Reaction

"The utmost exertion of your prudence will be necessary so as justly to temper your conduct between that caution and coolness which the delicacy of such a situation may demand, on the one hand, and the vigour necessary to suppress outrage and violence on the other."

—Secretary of state to colonial governors, October 1765

The story of British reaction to colonial resistance begins in mid-1765, taking place in parallel with colonial denial of parliamentary authority to tax the colonies, boycott, and the violent actions that prevented the act from going into effect. It was principally letters from Governors Fauquier, Bernard, Colden, and from General Gage that alerted the ministry to the dire situation in the colonies.

George Grenville was not destined to lead the reaction. As a consequence of personal and political matters (not related to his colonial policy) the king dismissed him. When speaking with the king on July 10, his last day in office, Grenville warned that the likely policy of the new ministry would be the "total subversion of every act" of Grenville's ministry "and most particularly on the regulations concerning the Colonies." He further advised the king

> not to suffer any one to advise him to separate or draw the line between his British and American dominions; that his Colonies was the richest jewel of his Crown [and] . . . that if any man ventured to defeat the regulations laid down for the Colonies by a slackness in the execution, he should look upon him as a criminal and the betrayer of his country.[1]

Grenville became leader of the opposition in Parliament. He advocated the enforcement of the Stamp Act in collaboration with his allies in the House of Lords, where there was little sympathy for conciliatory measures.

The situation in the months leading up to Grenville's dismissal was disruptive, complicated by personal and political considerations. A new ministry was eventually formed by the intervention and active role of the Duke of Cumberland, uncle of the king, who had made his mark as a military leader. Cumberland himself held no official position in the government, but for several months he was important in influencing the decisions of the ministry. His choice for head of the Treasury and first minister was the wealthy, young, and inexperienced (age thirty-five) Marquess of Rockingham. Although he had never played any significant government role, Rockingham had recently been under consideration for several ministerial positions, including as first lord of the Admiralty under Pitt. General Henry Seymour Conway, also inexperienced in civilian government, was established as secretary of state (southern department) and leader of the House of Commons; most other ministers chosen by Cumberland were similarly undistinguished. Rockingham was perceived as being indecisive, and as leading a weak government.[2] Even the king, after observing the ministry for the best part of a year, referred to them as "a few weak boys."[3] But agents and friends of America viewed the change positively. On July 16 Rhode Island agent Joseph Sherwood reported good news to Governor Ward: "I give you Joy on the Revolution in the Ministry. . . . It is confidently Asserted these Changes will produce great Ease to the Inhabitants of America."[4]

Although not himself becoming part of government, William Pitt played a role in the formation of the ministry. Pitt was the most distinguished statesman of the age as a result of his leading Great Britain to victory in the Seven Years' War (in addition, he was a brilliant orator, the most captivating speaker in the House of Commons). He was twice offered the opportunity to form a new government, but for complex reasons did not do so. Nevertheless, his influence over politically powerful men was so strong that his opinion had to be factored into any decision regarding the colonies.[5]

First news of a significant problem in the colonies—the Virginia Resolves—arrived shortly after the new government was formed. The June 5 letter from Lieutenant Governor Fauquier arrived on July 27, prompting a Board of Trade representation to the Privy Council on August 27.

> The resolutions, as they contain an absolute disavowal of the right of the parliament of Great-Britain to impose taxes upon her colonies, and a daring attack upon the constitution of this country, appear to us to require an immediate and serious attention. . . . [It may] be expedient to dispatch immediate instructions to your Majesty's servants in your Majesty's colony of Virginia . . . [that they support] the authority of parliament, vigorously exert themselves, and, with becoming resolution upon every occasion, exact a due obedience to all the laws of the land.[6]

The ministry did not wait for guidance from the king. Rockingham was influenced by Fauquier's statement that the resolutions were not the true "Sense of the Colony," and decided on August 30 only to write Fauquier a mild letter. The Privy Council met on September 6 but—the ministry having already made a decision about what action to take—did nothing more than defer the matter for further consideration. On September 14 Secretary of State Conway wrote Fauquier, assuring him that the king "and His Servants are satisfied" that no fault attached to him, but that the matter was under consideration by the Privy Council. "You will therefore, in the mean Time be very attentive by every prudent Measure in your Power, at once to maintain the just Rights of the British Government and to preserve the Peace and Tranquillity of the Province committed to your Care."[7] On the same day, the Treasury sent a circular letter to colonial governors (from Charles Lowndes) directing that they give "your aid and assistance to the Distributor of Stamps." (The letter arrived too late to influence action in the colonies.)

Reports from British officials were not the only source of information about attitudes and events in the colonies. Newspapers frequently printed reports of goings-on in the colonies, often without the delays of verification and confirmation of official reports. Here is news from Boston in the *London Evening Post* on September 14.

> New England, August 5, 1765
> As to the imposition of the stamp act (which takes place the 1st of November) it will, I believe, be of short continuance; for it is universally esteemed here as arbitrary and unconstitutional, and as a breach of charter and compact between K[ing] and subject; and we think we have a right to refuse submission to it. However, I believe most of the stamp masters will be afraid to act in such station as will stab their country. . . . It is too late in the day to be dragoon'd out of our rights.[8]

October was a stormy month in London. On October 1 the Board of Trade sent a representation to the Privy Council dealing with the letter of July 8 from Governor Bernard reporting the proposal for a congress of the colonies. The proposal was "without any previous application to your Majesty, to consider and deliberate upon the acts of the Parliament of this kingdom." However, the board offered no specific advice.

> As this appears to us to be the first instance of any general congress, appointed by the assemblies of the colonies without the authority of the crown . . . We therefore think it our indispensable duty to submit this matter to your Majesty's consideration, for such directions as your Majesty, with the advice of your council, may think proper and expedient to give thereupon.[9]

Particularly serious news began to arrive on October 5, demanding immediate attention. Bernard's letters of August 31 (arrived first), August 15–16, and August 22 brought news of the violent riots in Boston and the coerced resignation of the stamp distributor. The Treasury reacted quickly, directing Grey Cooper to write Bernard on October 8 that he "enforce a due Obedience to the Laws." The Bernard letters prompted additional representations from the Board of Trade to the Privy Council on October 10 and 17. The board expressed the opinion that the government in Massachusetts seems "to be utterly incapable of resisting or suppressing these tumults and disorders." The radical action seems "to us of such high importance that we lose no time in laying the letters and papers relating thereunto before your Majesty."[10]

It was also in October that the British came to a full realization that the Americans were not simply complaining about the burden of the tax. Whately wrote John Temple on October 11.

> I have not yet heard ye particulars of the disturbances in your Colony [i.e., the riots in Boston] but our printed accounts make them very great, & I am sure a little reflexion would convince the people that there is not the least foundation for their discontent. I do not find that ye tax itself is complain'd of, but ye opposition to it arises from a dispute of the right. Every principle of our Constitution & the uninterrupted practise of our legislature is against them.[11]

Whately wrote Grenville a week later.

> The rage of the people seems not to be confined to the Stamp Act; the Officers of the Customs are also the object of it, and if that should be avowed, then the clear point is whether the Parliament has a right to impose any taxes at all there.
>
> The language of the Ministry is, I am told, resolute, and they have certainly written to Governor Bernard, directing him to enforce the execution of the law vigorously, but I believe they are undetermined about the measures to be taken, and the mode of proceeding if the tumult continues.[12]

On October 18 the Privy Council, while still mulling over the reports of October 10 and 17, reacted to the Board of Trade reports of August 27 and October 1, reaching this conclusion.

> This is a Matter of the utmost Importance to the Kingdom and the Legislature of Great Britain, and of too high a Nature for the Determination of Your Majesty in Your Privy Council, and is proper only for the Consideration of Parliament.

In a further finding, the resolutions of Virginia were described as "containing an absolute Disavowal of the Right of the Parliament of Great Britain to impose Taxes upon the Colonies, and a daring attack upon the Constitution of this Country."[13]

On October 23, the Privy Council completed their evaluation of the two later Board of Trade reports and ordered the secretary of state to write the colonial governors with direction that they

> provide by all prudent and proper Methods for the Support of the Honour and Safety of Government, and use all legal means to preserve peace and good order by a full Exertion of the Civil Power, and in case by the Exigency of Affairs in any of the said Provinces, it should be necessary to procure the Aid of the Military in Support of the Civil Power, that, for that purpose, the Governor of the Province where that may happen, do apply to the Commanders of Your Majesty's Land and Sea Forces in America.[14]

The resulting letters from Secretary of State Conway are all dated October 24; they are vague and indecisive, with almost no true direction.

> It is with the greatest concern that his Majesty learns the disturbances which have arisen in some of the North American colonies. If this evil should spread to the government of __________, where you preside, the utmost exertion of your prudence will be necessary so as justly to temper your conduct

> between that caution and coolness which the delicacy of such a situation may demand, on the one hand, and the vigour necessary to suppress outrage and violence on the other.

Conway shows the degree to which he misunderstands the depth of American discontent.

> It is hoped and expected, that this want of confidence in the justice and tenderness of the mother country, and this open resistance to its authority, *can only have found place among the lower and more ignorant of the people.* The better and wiser part of the colonies will know that decency and submission may prevail, not only to redress grievances, but to obtain grace and favour, while the outrage of a public violence can expect nothing but severity and chastisement.

Here is equivocal guidance.

> If, by lenient and persuasive methods, you can contribute to restore that peace and tranquillity to the provinces, on which depend their welfare and happiness, you will do a most acceptable and essential service to your country: but having taken every step which the utmost prudence and lenity can dictate, in compassion to the *folly and ignorance of some misguided people*, you will not, on the other hand, fail to use your utmost power, for repelling all acts of outrage and violence, and to provide for the maintenance of peace and good order in the province, by such a timely exertion of force as the occasion may require: for which purpose, you will make the proper applications to general Gage, or lord Colvil[le], commanders of his Majesty's land and naval forces in America.[15]

A variant of the letter sent to Governor Bernard admonishes him.

> It is with the greatest Concern His Majesty learns the Disturbances, which have lately arisen in your Province; the general

> confusion that seems to reign there; and the total Languor and want of Energy in your Government to exert itself with any Dignity or Efficacy for the Suppression of Tumults.[16]

Although the letters mention "exertion of force," perhaps implying approval to use military power to enforce the Stamp Act, no such policy decision had been made; the ministry continued undetermined about measures to be taken. In any event, no governor took action as a result of the letter.

October 28 saw arrival of the letters of September 23 from New York (Colden, dealing with "a secret Correspondence" and from Gage, "Signal for a general outcry" and "the almost general Resignation of the Stamp Officers"), increasing the level of trepidation about the colonies by making it clear that the violence was not spontaneous mob action but rather was planned continent-wide resistance. Had these letters arrived a week earlier they are likely to have led Conway to be more assertive in demanding action from the governors.

The growing crisis demanded immediate action by the ministry; accordingly, Rockingham scheduled a cabinet meeting at the home of the Duke of Cumberland on October 31—a meeting never held because of the duke's sudden death that day. The meeting would have unveiled one minister's plan that "the Stamp Act ought to be carried into Execution in support of the Sovereignty of the British Parl[iamen]t over the Colonies." Further, that governors should be directed to enforce execution of the act and be "furnished with the Assistance of a Military Force for this Purpose."[17] Cumberland was likely to have supported such strong measures, and his death may well have affected the direction taken by the ministry, even the trajectory of events of the Stamp Act crisis. Prior to his death there had been no indication that the ministry was seriously considering concession. Shortly after the repeal of the Stamp Act, Richard Jackson claimed "that if the Duke of Cumberland had not died, instead of a repeal of the Act, there wou'd have been a number of Regiments in America before this."[18]

Despite the known tendency of Cumberland, the public posture assumed by the ministry was that his death would have no effect on policy. Whatley informed Grenville on November 8 that "the adherents to the Ministry treat it as an event of no consequence, for that he took no part in the conduct of affairs."[19] The death of Cumberland and the closing optimistic comment from Gage in his letter of September 23 ("calm seems to have succeeded the Storm") led the ministry to postpone any decision until learning of the American reaction on November 1.

News of the convening of the congress at New York reached London on November 15 in the October 12 letter from General Gage that ended with another optimistic assessment that the act "may be introduced without much Difficulty in several of the Colonys, and if it is began in some, that it will soon spread over the rest." That viewpoint allayed fears of rebellion and led the ministry to continue deferring any action.

December 10 was a troubling day. The letter of November 5 from Lieutenant Governor Colden about the riot of November 1 arrived (carried by Major James, who further described the New York situation to General Conway), plus two letters from General Gage. His observation of November 4 about the need for a "considerable military force" made it clear that enforcement was not an attractive option, and his letter of November 8 about ("terrifying the stamp officers . . . has been compleated throughout") reinforced the realization of continent-wide resistance. The ministry was at a loss for what to do.

Secretary of State Conway responded on December 15 to the Gage letters. He laments "with the utmost concern, the disordered state of the province where you reside, and the very riotous and outrageous behaviour of too many of the inhabitants." He offers these platitudes.

> Your situation is certainly delicate and difficult; it requires both prudence and firmness in the conduct of all employed in his Majesty's service there; especially, considering what you say of the difficulty, or rather impossibility, of drawing any considerable number of men together, and of the impracticability of attempting any thing by force, in the present disposition of the people, without a respectable body of troops.

General Conway is sympathetic to the military situation facing General Gage, but he can only offer more platitudes.

> You seem to think there are still hopes, that as the spirits of those unhappy people have time to cool, there will be more submission shewn. . . . [nonetheless] exert yourself where the necessity of the case may require, in support of the honour of government, and for suppressing any riotous or rebellious resistance offered to the laws.[20]

Conway wrote Colden the same day with still more platitudes.

> From your last letter, I have hopes that time will produce a recollection, which may lead these unhappy people back to a sense of their duty; and that, in the mean time, every proper and practicable measure will be taken to awe that licentious spirit, which has hurried them to those acts of outrage and violence, equally dangerous to the sober and well-disposed part of the people, the ease and quiet of the city, and subversive of all order and authority among them.[21]

On December 17, the Board of Trade provided the Privy Council more information (letters from Governor Bernard) describing the collapse of British authority in Massachusetts. The report highlighted Bernard's despondent "P.S. of Nov. 8" that "there is such an appearance of tranquillity that I may remain here a cipher some time longer."[22] Before the end of December it had become clear that British government in the colonies was in a shambles.

Ten

Decision

"The Ideas we join in are nearly what I talked of to you this morning. That is—a Declaratory Act—in General Terms afterwards to proceed to Considerations of Trade etc.—and finally Determination on the Stamp Act—ie—a Repeal, and which its own Demerits and Inconveniences felt here will justify."

—Rockingham to Yorke, January 1766

THE MINISTRY FACED a difficult decision on policy: a choice between concession—repeal, modification, or suspension—and enforcement. Any serious retreat would be seen as a surrender to colonial resistance, a weakness that diminished the authority of Parliament over the colonies. Enforcement would require the use of military force, likely leading to civil war and conflict with British enemies in Europe. The ministry being unable to make a decision without knowing what Pitt would advocate, 1765 ended in uncertainty, the only fixed star being that the right of Parliament to tax the colonies could not be forsaken. But in early 1766, following a forceful call for repeal of the Stamp Act from Pitt, the ministry reached a decision: repeal the Stamp Act with a strategy based on economic benefit to Great Britain.

Trade is Disrupted

Beginning late in 1764, the distress in the colonies was becoming increasingly known in Great Britain and was soon to affect the British economy.

News From the Colonies

In September 1764, the *London Chronicle* reported news of remonstrances from the colonies "with respect to their crampt trade." The London *Gentleman's Magazine* reported that "the New Commercial regulations in North America are complained of as grievous to the colonies."[1] The situation was even more distressing in 1765 after news reached America about passage of the Stamp Act. On June 6, the London *St. James Chronicle* printed extracts from New York letters that reported the Stamp Act was called "the Folly of England and the Ruin of America" and reported two days later that orders from colonial merchants for goods were "countermanded, on account of the new American Stamp Duties." By early August the news contained quotes of American denials of the authority of Parliament.[2] On August 10, a letter from Virginia dated June 5 was published in *Felix Farley's Bristol Journal*. The writer (alluding to the Virginia Resolves) addressed the feelings of Americans, objecting to the "shackles" placed on "the American colonies, by the imposition of the stamp duties." The writer shouts out his purpose, "that the people of England may be informed, in some sort, of our dismal situation." By the end of the year the New York nonimportation agreement had been published in Bristol.[3]

In addition to hearing public news about the situation in America, merchants were receiving anxious letters directly from their American counterparts about "the low Ebb of Trade," and that the Stamp Act will worsen the situation: "we shall not be able much longer to support trade." Most disturbing, calling for action, British merchants heard the outcry, "I wonder the merchants and friends to America don't make some stir for us."[4]

Great Britain

Even before passage of the Stamp Act many British merchants in

1764 were sympathetic to the difficult situation of trade in the colonies as a result of the Sugar Act. The *London Chronicle* reported in September 1764 that "they write from Bristol, that the principal merchants of that city intend to support with all their interest the independent free trade of the North American colonies." It was in 1765 however, that British merchants began to suffer the consequences of colonial distress. Henry Cruger Jr., born in America but now an important merchant doing business in Bristol, wrote Aaron Lopez (a merchant in Newport, Rhode Island) on September 13. "Money is so scarce in the Kingdom, and trade of all sorts so dull." Cruger wrote Lopez again on October 4: "Trade is as much at a stand in England as in America; my Friends in London write me they know not what to do with their Ships." On October 26, the *St. James's Chronicle* reported the drop in exports to America as "near 600,000£ less this Summer, than has been known for 30 years past." By the end of 1765, orders countermanded specifically because of the Stamp Act were reported as 700,000 Sterling. In October, the Society of Merchant Venturers of Bristol prepared a petition to the Treasury protesting "the restraints laid upon the navigation in America, not only by the commanders of his majesty's ships of war but also by the patent officers there who exercise their authority with the exceeding great vigour."[5]

On December 28, a Bristol merchant printed a letter he had received from Maryland countermanding an earlier order. He expressed his reasons for having the letter printed.

> that it may be instrumental in opening the eyes of the public, *and by their means the legislature*, to the TRUE INTEREST of the nation; and the hardships to which that Act has subjected, not only the English merchants trading to America, but many thousands of manufacturers depending thereon for bread.[6]

The letter is explicit—such an effect usually not being mentioned—that opening the eyes of the public would be tantamount to gaining the attention of Parliament.

Steps Toward a Decision

On November 6, Benjamin Franklin met with the president of the Board of Trade, Lord Dartmouth. Franklin wrote to his son, New Jersey governor William Franklin, on November 9: "I gave it to him as my Opinion, that the general Execution of the Stamp Act would be impracticable without occasioning more Mischief than it was worth." He also argued that Britain could use the expected address from the congress at New York as a reason to suspend the act—and then later drop it "without ever bringing the Question of Right to a Decision." Further, "that to send Armies & Fleets to enforce the Act, would not, in my Opinion, answer any good End." Dartmouth did not think Parliament would accept the products of the congress at New York.

> Some Difficulty would arise about receiving it, as it was an irregular Meeting, unauthoriz'd by any American Constitution. I said, I hoped Government here would not be too nice on that Head; That the Mode was indeed new, but to the People there it seem'd necessary, *their separate Petitions last Year being rejected*. And to refuse hearing Complaints and Redressing Grievances, from Punctilios about Form, had always an ill Effect.

Franklin realizes that there is a major political problem associated with repeal: "It is true that Inconveniences may arise to Government here by a Repeal of the Act, as it will be deem'd a tacit giving up the Sovereignty of Parliament." However, Franklin continues, "I think the Inconveniences of persisting much greater." He sees the political situation facing the ministry.

> The present Ministry are truely perplex'd how to act on the Occasion: as, if they relax, their Predecessors will reproach them with giving up the Honour, Dignity, and Power of this Nation.[7]

Richard Jackson wrote Governor Bernard on November 8: "I confess cannot foresee what government will do here, but am informed they are determined to support the stamp act, and not to give way to its repeal."[8] Jackson's perception changes quickly, writing Governor Fitch on November 15.

> I have within ye Compass of a week conceived hopes, that Measures may be taken here, that will perfectly conciliate ye minds of ye Americans, but . . . yet depend upon ye Moderation of what we hear from New York.

But more is needed.

> In a Parlt [referring to passage of the Stamp Act] where but 49 voted agt a Bill in ye H of C & which passed unanimously in ye H of L, it cannot reasonably be expected ye Bill shd be [easily] repealed.[9]

On November 28, Rockingham jotted down some rough notes for himself dealing with a "Plan of Business" for the upcoming Parliamentary session. He realized that it would be important "to avoid the discussion on the Stamp Act—till Good Principles are laid down for Easing and Assisting N[orth] America and being well informed of the high Importance of the Commerce [of the colonies] . . . to the Mother Country."[10] Rockingham by this time was—regardless of varied opinions held by other ministers—leaning toward some form of compromise. Grenville had this view of the situation, writing the Duke of Bedford that "they [the ministry] are resolved, if possible, to repeal the American tax."[11]

Rockingham had come to realize that the distress of the merchants might lead Parliament to conciliation, and that an alliance with the merchants might lay the foundation for "Easing and Assisting" the colonies. His method of highlighting problems of economic distress—and of pointing to a solution—was to work in concert with those who were already finding fault with the Stamp Act and expressing support for "the independent free trade of the North American colonies." His principal contact was Barlow Trecothick, a wealthy merchant and prominent figure in American trade. By December 4,

Trecothick had organized and become chairman of a committee of merchants of London trading to North America. At a general meeting of London merchants, the committee was given this charge.

> Consider of the best Method of Application for Procuring the Relief and Encouragement of the North American trade, and to apply to the Outports and to the Manufacturing Citys and Towns for their Concurrence and Assistance.[12]

On December 6, the committee sent a letter to the port and manufacturing towns: The "Maritime and manufacturing Part of these Kingdoms must be affected by the Distresses of North American Commerce," and we ask, "your Concurrence and Assistance in Support of a regular application to Parliament." They continue,

> We desire to unite with you in a Measure so essential to the best Interests of Great Britain, wishing to have your Sentiments on the Subject, thro' the Course of which we mean to take for our guide the Interests of these Kingdoms—it being our Opinion, that conclusive Arguments for granting every Ease or Advantage the North-Americans can with Propriety desire, may be fairly deduced from that Principle only.[13]

That redress of colonial grievances can be justified strictly based on the "Interests of these Kingdoms" is an early manifestation of what will become the bedrock of Rockingham's strategy for repeal. The idea behind the closing words is that it was unnecessary—and unwise—to bring up constitutional issues or any other aspect of American resistance to the Stamp Act. Trecothick later testified before Parliament that the intent was "to make the interest of Great Britain the Basis of their application."[14]

Recently appointed Massachusetts agent Dennys De Berdt (an aging but influential merchant) wrote on December 14 of positive news for the colonies: "I have the pleasure to acquaint you the ministry are intirely convinced of the Bad Tendency of the late regulations & disposed to relieve you."

> I have further the satisfaction to Inform you that the merchants of London are warmly espous[ing] your Cause [and] have chosen a Committee to Carry on an application to parliament. [The committee has] sent Circular Letters to the Principal Cities & Towns throughout the Kingdom to Join their Weight and influence with ours & then to Bring Both City & Country [as] well as your own Petittions in aid to the ministry.[15]

When the House of Commons opened on December 17, the purpose was routine business: to issue writs of election to fill vacancies caused by members becoming ministers (hence being required to stand for reelection). The ministry intended the king's speech to downplay the American reaction to the Stamp Act, making this incredible understatement: "*Matters of importance* have lately occurred in some of my colonies in America, which will demand the most serious attention of parliament." The proposed address of thanks also skirted the problems. However, the session became the first parliamentary battleground for dealing with American resistance. Grenville launched an attack (planned in advance and accompanied by a similar move in the House of Lords) on what he saw as a timid response to American resistance; he proposed this amendment.

> To express our just resentment and indignation at the outrageous tumults and insurrections which have been excited and carried on in North America, and at the resistance given by open and rebellious force, to the execution of the laws in that part of his Majesty's dominions.

This was followed by advocacy of "all such measures as shall be necessary for . . . enforcing their due obedience to the laws" in order to maintain the "fundamental rights of the legislature of Great Britain." The motion was debated for several hours; it being implicitly understood that such enforcement would require military force. The tide going against him, Grenville withdrew the amendment. Similar action occurred in the House of Lords.[16]

On December 24, Edward Sedgwick explained that he is "full of Anxiety with regard to the Consequences of the American dispute."

> The Evil is in all respects of such a Magnitude, that I cannot presume to guess what are the Measures proper to be pursued for remedying it. The only thing I am clear in, & that I have been from the beginning, is, that the Right of the British Legislature to tax the Colonies is clear and incontestable, and that it must not, cannot be given up, without annihilating the British Constitution in British America.[17]

Rockingham held informal meetings in December, often including his confidantes outside the ministry. It was at two meetings of December 27 and 31 that many ideas were discussed that eventually became part of the ministry strategy. On January 2, 1766, Rockingham wrote to the Duke of Newcastle to summarize the meetings.

> I think one thing seems to be the General opinion—that is—that the *Legislative Right of this Country* over the Colonies—should be declared—and upon the Plan of Act The 6th of Geo[rge] the 1st relative to Ireland. I think it also seemed the General Opinion—that in the King's Speech and in all the Parliamentary Proceedings—the Intention of giving the Colonies every possible Relief in Trade and Commerce should go hand in hand with declarations of Authority or Censures of the Riots and Tumults.

(The phrasing of the "Legislative Right of this Country" was eventually based on the Irish Declaratory Act of 1719. It asserted that Parliament had "full power and authority to make laws and statutes of sufficient validity to bind the Kingdom and people of Ireland." Significantly, Parliament never relied on the act to impose taxes on the Irish.)

The idea of emphasizing the authority of Parliament coupled with "every possible relief" was the starting point for the decisions the ministry would make in the coming weeks—after hearing what Pitt had to say.

> The main matter in which as yet I can not see exactly where and how the different opinions can be brought to agree—is—what must finally be done upon the Stamp Act. All would agree to various Amendments and Curtailings of the Act—some as yet not very many to a Suspension and Very Few to a Repeal. Your Grace knows that among even ourselves there are difference of Opinions.[18]

On January 11, Richard Jackson explained his view of the situation to Governor Fitch.

> I am informed by the best Intelligence I can procure that the Stamp Act will not be repealed; every other Relief may be, I think, expected, and even this Law will probably be reduced to nothing more than a proof of the power of Parliament to impose taxes as well as make other laws for America. Something to assert this power is judged necessary by leading men in both Houses; I wish that some other means of attaining the same end may be thought of rather than this, but I fear no other will.[19]

On January 13, the day before the topic of American resistance was scheduled to come before Parliament, the most persistent of the ministry's critics (going by the pseudonym of Anti-Sejanus) made this comment in *Lloyd's Evening Post*. He wrote, if "our timid and ill-judging Ministers intend to give way to the tumultous Americans, can it be supposed that the Colonists will ever submit to bear any share in those grievous burdens and taxes, with which we are loaded?"[20]

Pitt Becomes an Advocate

Parliament reopened on January 14. The king's speech asserted Parliament's constitutional authority; it encouraged "attention to the just Rights and Authority of the British Legislature" and stressed the need for "the Assertion of legal Authority [and] . . . the Equity and good Order of My Government." The address of thanks addressed "zeal for the Honour of His Majesty's Government" and similar expressions, balanced by "the utmost Attention to the important Objects of the Trade and Navigation of these Kingdoms."[21]

The resulting debate on the address of thanks immediately skewed away from the address itself to deal with the relationship between Britain and America.[22] Robert Nugent, a follower of Grenville, started the discussion. He was insistent that "the honour and dignity of the kingdom obliged us to compel the execution of the Stamp Act, except the right was acknowledged, and the repeal solicited as a favour." The "produce of the Stamp Act" would not be great, but,

> *A pepper-corn in acknowledgment of the right was of more value than millions without.* He expatiated on the extreme ingratitude of the Colonies; and concluded with charging the ministry with encouraging petitions to parliament, and instructions to members from the trading and manufacturing towns, against the Act.

The charge of "encouraging petitions" was the beginning of a series of claims by the opposition that such encouragement was deceitful, that the petitions were an invention of the ministry.

Pitt then rose and gave perfunctory approval of the address of thanks, then set the tone for the rest of his speech, publicly revealing for the first time his position on taxation and the proper way to deal with the colonies.

> It is my opinion that this kingdom has no right to lay a tax upon the colonies. At the same time, I assert the authority of this kingdom over the colonies to be sovereign and supreme, in every circumstance of government and legislation whatsoever. They are the subjects of this kingdom; equally entitled with yourselves to all the natural rights of mankind and the peculiar privileges of Englishmen; equally bound by its laws, and equally participating in the constitution of this free country. The Americans are the sons, not the bastards of England! *Taxation is no part*

> *of the governing or legislative power.* The taxes are a voluntary gift and grant of the Commons alone.

He emphasized that such a gift of the commons was inappropriate.

> But in an American tax, what do we do? We, your Majesty's Commons for Great Britain, give and grant to your Majesty, what? Our own property?—No. We give and grant to your Majesty, the property of your Majesty's Commons of America! It is an absurdity in terms.

He asserted that "the distinction between legislation and taxation is essentially necessary to liberty," then turned to virtual representation. His conclusion was that "the idea of a virtual representation of America in this House is the most contemptible idea that ever entered into the head of a man—it does not deserve a serious refutation." He emphasized that the American exclusive right of taxation is based on representation.

> The Commons of America, represented in their several assemblies, have ever been in possession of the exercise of this, their constitutional right, of giving and granting their own money. They would have been slaves if they had not enjoyed it.

Nonetheless, he emphasized that "this kingdom, as the supreme governing and legislative power, has always bound the colonies by her laws, by her regulations, and restrictions in trade, in navigation, in manufactures, in everything except that of taking their money out of their pockets without their consent."

Conway praised Pitt, seeming to commit the ministry to Pitt's position, stating his "own sentiments were entirely conformable to those of the Right Honorable Gentleman."

Grenville responded with criticism of the ministry.

> The disturbances in America began in July, and now we are in the middle of January; lately they were only occurrences; they

> are now grown to disturbances, to tumults, and riots . . . and if the doctrine I have heard this day be confirmed . . . a revolution will take place in America.

He addressed the form of taxation that was to be placed on the colonists.

> I cannot understand the difference between external and internal taxes. They are the same in effect, and differ only in name. That this kingdom has the sovereign, the supreme legislative power over America, is granted. It cannot be denied; and *taxation is a part of that Sovereign power.*

He stated that "Protection and obedience are reciprocal. Great-Britain protects America; America is bound to yield obedience." But he complained that when "they are called upon to contribute a small share towards the public expense . . . they renounce your authority, insult your officers, and break out, I might almost say, in open rebellion."

Pitt spoke in rebuttal.

> The gentleman tells us, America is obstinate; America is almost in open rebellion. I rejoice that America has resisted. Three millions of people, so dead to all feelings of liberty, as voluntarily to submit to be slaves, would have been fit instruments to make slaves of the rest.

He went on to ridicule Grenville.

> If the gentleman does not understand the difference between internal and external taxes, I cannot help it; but there is a plain distinction between taxes levied for the purposes of raising a revenue, and duties imposed for the regulation of trade, for the accommodation of the subject; although, in the consequences, some revenue might incidentally arise from the latter.

Pitt responded to the charge that, regarding protection, Americans renounce Parliament's authority: "The profits to Great Britain from the trade of the colonies, through all its branches, is two millions a year. This is the fund that carried you triumphantly through the last war. . . . *You owe this to America: this is the price America pays you for her protection.*" He ended with elaboration of his opening statement, essentially defining a strategy for repeal.

> Upon the whole, I will beg leave to tell the House what is really my opinion. It is that the Stamp Act be repealed absolutely, totally, and immediately. That the reason for the repeal be assigned, because it was founded on an erroneous principle. At the same time, let the sovereign authority of this country over the colonies be asserted in as strong terms as can be devised, and be made to extend to every point of legislation whatsoever. That we may bind their trade, confine their manufactures, and exercise every power whatsoever, except that of taking their money out of their pockets without their consent!

A brief summarization of Pitt's speech, in a letter from James West who consistently made reports of speeches in the House of Commons to the Duke of Newcastle, interprets Pitt as dealing with internal taxation.

> [Pitt declared] that the Act ought to be totally and absolutely repealed as an erroneous policy, that no Treasury ever had thought of taxing America in the most necessitous times, that the Parliament had no power to enact an *internal taxation* in America.[23]

All in all, the debate went far beyond anything necessary to agree on the mild and uncontroversial address of thanks, which, almost incidentally, was approved.

Massachusetts agent Dennys De Berdt, reporting on January 16, interpreted Pitt's position as being directed to internal taxation: "Mr. Pitt in a long Speach opened in our favour silenced all the objections of the old Ministry & asserted yr. right of Internal Taxation in the strongest Terms."[24] South Carolina agent Charles Garth, writing on January 19, also viewed Pitt as denying Parliament the right of internal taxation.

> What the issue will be I protest I know not, from the Speech & Address it looks as if the Intention of the Ministry was at that time for palliating Measures only, but Mr. Pitt having declared his Opinion against the Right of Parliament to impose an Internal Tax and for that reason if for no other that the Stamp Act ought to be repeal'd, *I should think the Ministry must adopt that Plan.*[25]

Others saw things differently, *that Pitt rejected all taxation.* Sir Edward Turner voiced the viewpoint common in the large voting bloc of country gentleman—those who sat in the House of Commons on their own account, beholden neither to the Crown nor any patron, and who paid large land taxes. Turner was a wealthy investor as well as a member of the House of Commons and was close to Grenville and Jenkinson. He voted against repeal of the Stamp Act. He wrote to a friend on January 18.

> Mr. Pitt's opinion . . . that Great Britain hath no right to tax the Colonies, cannot convince me or many others of inferior, common, and unrefined understandings. If that Right be given up (but I think it impossible) good by America![26]

Yet others in the House of Commons thought Pitt's stance to be obscure, seeing a muddle between internal and external taxes and their relationship to duties for raising revenue and duties for regulation of trade. The ministry took advantage of the ambiguity to lead Parliament toward a belief that Americans did not object to all taxes, only internal taxes such as the Stamp Act.

The Decision

On January 19, Rockingham met in the morning with Attorney General Charles Yorke, then in the evening with other close advisors. He brought Yorke up to date.

> The Ideas we join in are nearly what I talked of to you this morning. That is—a *Declaratory Act*—in General Terms afterwards to proceed to *Considerations of Trade* etc.—and finally *Determination on the Stamp Act—ie—a Repeal*, and which its own Demerits and Inconveniences *felt here* will justify.[27]

The decision became easy to make after Pitt had advocated repeal in no uncertain terms. The ministry took its own path however, and discarded Pitt's unpopular ideas. The purpose of repeal is not "erroneous principle," and the strategy rejects his statement "that this kingdom has no right to lay a tax upon the colonies." Rockingham stressed the importance of "considerations of trade" and that economic distress in Britain ("felt here") is the foundation for repeal.

Over the next few days the ministry developed five resolutions to support the repeal strategy. The first four made assertions about the situation in the colonies and remedial actions: (1) that dangerous tumults and insurrections had taken place in the colonies; (2) that several colonial assemblies had encouraged such insurrections; (3) that perpetrators of the "riots and insurrections" must be punished; and (4) that compensation should be provided to those who have suffered as a result of the riots and insurrections. The fifth resolution was the most important: the declaration of right as a basis for a declaratory act proclaiming the authority of Parliament over the colonies, essentially the declaration in "general terms" that had been agreed on January 19. Charles Yorke thought the resolutions were not forceful enough to satisfy the House of Lords. He suggested modifications, the most significant (shown in brackets) was to the fifth resolution.

> Resolved, That the Parliament of Great Britain had, hath, and of a right ought to have, full power and authority to make laws and statutes of sufficient force and validity to bind the Colonies and people of America in all cases whatsoever [as well in cases of Taxation, as in all other cases whatsoever].[28]

Rockingham wrote Yorke on the evening of January 25.

> General Conway having sent to me the proposed Resolutions with some alterations which you have made, I cannot help troubling you with my doubts upon some of them. The Resolutions in general exceed in spirit what the generality of our friends wish, but, in expectation that coming into them will pave the way for the actual repeal of the Stamp Act, I think they will be agreed to.

Here is the most telling comment, the refusal to add the dreaded word.

> The . . . alteration which I particularly object to, is the insertion of "taxation" and I think I may say that it is our firm resolution in the House of Lords (I mean among ourselves) *that that word must not be inserted*.[29]

At some point toward the end of January, Conway explained to Massachusetts agent Dennys De Berdt the situation as seen by the ministry.

> Mr. Conway told me there was 3 Parties in the House: one was [for enforcement] the other for a Repeal but for previous resolves to assert the right & Power of Parliament. The Third, which Includes the ministry, for a Repeal without any previous resolutions at all. But *in Order to secure the Repeal* they were obliged to agree to the resolves in order to secure a majority for a Repeal.[30]

Conway overstated the degree of consensus in the ministry, but his explanation of the need for resolutions of "right & Power" made it clear that the resolves were established not as a matter of principle but as a political statement.

THE DECISION ON POLICY and strategy was set: repeal, with the reason being correction of the economic distress in Britain; the repeal to be accompanied by a strong statement of the authority of Parliament.

Eleven

Repeal of the Stamp Act

"The Repeal of this Law, under the present Circumstances, will, we fear, not only surrender the Honour and essential Interests of the Kingdom, now and for ever, both at Home and Abroad, but will also deeply affect the fundamental Principles of our Constitution."

—Dissent in the House of Lords, March 17, 1766

THE DECISION having been made to repeal the Stamp Act with a strategy based on economic benefit to Great Britain, Rockingham in early 1766 faced the practical matter of gathering the necessary votes. He chose to implement the strategy using evidence from merchants and manufacturers of the economic harm they had suffered because of the Stamp Act, and that only repeal would correct the problem. In addition, to avoid any impression of surrender to colonial demands, the repeal was to be accompanied by an assertion of the full power and authority of Parliament to legislate (laws and statutes) for the colonies. A subtle additional aspect of swaying Parliament to repeal was to create the impression that the colonies denied only internal taxation, not all parliamentary authority to tax the colonies. Such an impression (a flawed representation of American beliefs, and one that Rockingham needed to develop carefully, even surreptitiously) would make arguments against taxation less objectionable than a wholesale rejection of Parliament's authority. In support of that strategy, it was necessary to hide, or at least downplay, American denial of the taxation authority of Parliament.

In the end, the Stamp Act was repealed, not as a surrender to the often violent American resistance, not as an admission that it violated the rights of the colonists, but rather as an act that was inexpedient at the time and was "attended with many inconveniencies."

Building a Foundation for Repeal

On January 17, the first of the petitions from the merchants was presented to the House of Commons: the "Petition of the Merchants of London, trading to North America."

> The petitioners have been long concerned in carrying on the trade between this country and the British colonies on the continent of North America; and that they have annually exported very large quantities of British manufactures . . . by all which many thousand manufacturers, seamen and labourers, have been employed, to the very great and increasing benefit of this nation.

The petition described the nature of the trade, ending with

> [Trade] must be deemed of the highest importance in the commercial system of this nation; and that this commerce, so beneficial to the state, and so necessary for the support of multitudes, now lies under such difficulties and discouragement, that nothing less than its utter ruin is apprehended, without the immediate interposition of parliament.

It went on by saying that the existing debts were at risk because of the past actions of Parliament.

> [The colonies are] indebted to the merchants of Great Britain in the sum of several millions sterling; and that at this time the

> colonists, when pressed for payment [allege] that the taxes and restrictions laid upon them, and the extension of the jurisdiction of vice admiralty courts established by some late acts of parliament . . . disturb legal commerce [to the point that] the former opportunities and means of remittances and payments are utterly lost and taken from them.

It ends "praying the consideration of the premises, and entreating such relief, as to the House shall seem expedient."[1]

On January 21, petitions prepared by the agents of Virginia (Montague) and Georgia (Knox) were presented to the House. Garth explained that "the mention of the matter of Right was avoided at the [insistence] of the Ministry, who . . . were desirous of having the debate upon the Point of Right postponed, matters being then not quite Ripe for that purpose." The ministry dealt with the issue by referring the petitions to the American Committee.[2]

Dealing with the petition of the Stamp Act Congress was tricky business. Rockingham did not want to bring it to the formal attention of the House of Commons since doing so would bring out that the Americans were specific in objecting to all taxation. Political factors intervened however, and a motion to bring up the petition in the House was made on January 27. Garth explained that the first objection was to form, the petition being improperly signed. But Garth knew such objection was largely a pretext: "Another Objection was that it partook too much of a Federal Union assembled without any requisition on the part of the supreme Power." But the greatest threat was to the laws of trade.

> A third Objection [was] that it tended to Question not only the Rights of Parliament to impose internal Taxes, but external Duties, both being blended together as necessary to be repeal'd.

The ministry could not support

> a petition questioning the Power in the Case of Duties necessary for the Regulation of Trade, which went to the very vitals

> of the Legislative Authority, & strongly pointed at Independency upon the Mother Country.

After much debate, the ministry—wishing to have the petition neither read nor explicitly rejected—"mov'd about eleven at Night for the Order of the Day, which was agreed to and in that manner the Fate of that Petition determined."[3] Conway later explained to the king that he "thought the temper of the house was much against the Petition & that it would have been a Bad Question to have our first Division upon."[4] The appeal addressed to the House of Lords was also rejected on a matter of form "because it was memorial which that House never accepts."[5]

On January 28, the American Committee began reading papers and hearing testimony. Garth continues his story, writing on February 9.

> Very sorry I am to observe that the Contents of many of the papers particularly from the Northern Colonies, touching the Legislative Authority of Parliament . . . were receiv'd by the Committee with an Impression far from favourable to the great Object in View.
>
> It is very unfortunate that the Steps to prevent the Acts taking place were in some places carried to that length and extremity they have been. . . . I mention this because I think it has in some sort hurt the Cause, not only in the House of Commons, but very much in the House of Lords.[6]

Martin Howard Jr., a prominent attorney and political conservative from Rhode Island, provided insight into the overall situation in America. As part of a discursive answer to a question about the violence in Newport, he observed that the colonial "discontent showed itself but lately." The Americans "made no Objection while they [were] only Taxed by Customs [i.e., duties on trade]. But now the whole [i.e., object to all taxes]." The diversion prompted more questions about American opinions: "Did you ever [hear] of any objections to the jurisdiction of the Parliament before the Sugar Act took place?" He answered, "Never. The establishing ships [i.e., use of the

British navy to enforce the laws of trade] gave great objection." Asked if the Americans object to the Navigation Act, he answered, "They do not extend it so far."

Major James, the commander of Fort George during the New York riot of November 1, testified that the discontent in New York resulted in a "mob of 3 or 4000 people," which he opposed with a defensive force of 151 men. He explained that "if I had fired, I should have killed 900 of them." But this would have raised "a general resistance. In two days more there would have been 20,000 strong." He added that "there can be assembled in New York and the Jerseys 50,000 [American] fighting men."[7]

Declaratory Resolution in Committee

On February 3, the ministry introduced their five resolutions in the American committees of the Lords and Commons. The declaratory resolution was the first to be addressed in order to start the day on a matter of broad agreement.

> That the King's Majesty, by and with the Advice and Consent of the Lords Spiritual and Temporal, and Commons, of Great Britain, in Parliament assembled, had, hath, and of Right ought to have, full Power and Authority to make Laws and Statutes, of sufficient Force and Validity to bind the Colonies and People of America, Subjects of the Crown of Great Britain, in all Cases whatsoever.[8]

In the House of Commons, Conway established the foundation for the ministry's resolutions, beginning by criticizing colonial actions but blaming Grenville's legislation for the economic depression of the colonies. He ended that "he never was nor ever shall be a friend to internal taxation in America. He does not deny the legal right, but he thinks [that as a] point of policy and justice this ought not to have been attempted." He read the five resolutions and moved to adopt the first.[9]

Hans Stanley, a follower of Grenville, supported the declaratory resolution but viewed it as incompatible with the expected later plan to repeal the Stamp Act. (He opposed repeal, favoring modification.) "If this resolution is only specious, we shall give up all authority over the Americans and can never possibly recover it without all the miseries of a civil war." He feared the danger

> is not approaching but actually begun. . . . They have begun a Federal Union. . . . The repeal of the Stamp Act will not content the Americans. A few years, or rather a few months, will bring them again before you with . . . opposition to your whole system of laws of American legislation.

Charles Yorke disagreed with Stanley about the incompatibility of the declaration and repeal of the act; he viewed the declaration as being "not inconsistent with your own dignity and with that temper which becomes this great assembly upon such an occasion. *We separate the question of right from the question of expediency.*"

After further debate, Isaac Barre, at 10:15 p.m., moved to have the words "in all cases whatever" [i.e., whatsoever] left out." He supported taxation only with consent, based on the concept that "the supreme power is uncontrollable, but it should control itself." Any internal tax could be enforced only by military might. If Britain did so, the Americans would submit, but with dire consequences.

> All colonies have their date of independence. The wisdom or folly of our conduct may make it sooner or later. If we act injudiciously, this point may be reached in the life of many of the members of this House.

Barre ended with this rationale for deleting the offensive phrase: "The words 'in all cases whatever' will destroy their confidence in you, which gentler resolution and gentler measure may obtain."

After yet more debate it was after midnight when Pitt spoke as a second for Barre's motion. The resulting lengthy discussion clarified that the vague phrase "in all cases whatsoever" was interpreted by Parliament to include taxation. Garth described the conclusion.

> The Debate ended about 4 in the Morning, when the Question was put in Consequence of Col. Barre's Motion "that the words in all Cases whatever stand part of the Resolution," I believe from the Sound there were not more than ten dissenting voices.

Garth was one of the dissenting voices (largely consisting of Pitt and a few friends) but nonetheless was pleased with the debate.

> A fuller House I dont recollect to have seen, and it is to the Honour of Parliament I must add, that I believe there never was a debate so Temperate, serious, Solemn and Parliamentary, without the least appearance of Party or faction (disunited and divided as we are) intermingling in the Arguments upon the Question on one side or other.[10]

In the Lords there was a two-hour discussion with little disagreement; the declaratory resolution was carried 125 to 5.[11]

The ministry lost no time making the news available; it was published the morning of February 5 in the popular London newspaper *Gazetteer and New Daily Advertiser.*

> As we are informed it is now decided that the legislature of this Kingdom hath a right to levy taxes on America, we beg leave to inform our correspondents that we can no longer admit any letters in which that right is in any wise controverted. While it was an undecided question, we readily admitted the disputants on either side of it; but since it is no longer so, our correspondents must submit to that august decision.[12]

The following days in Parliament saw resolutions being defeated or modified, and amendments and new resolutions being proposed and agreed. In the end there were six resolutions approved, the most significant being the first, the declaratory resolution.[13] There was as yet no proposed resolution for the repeal.

A Turning Point

On February 7, Grenville introduced a motion in committee similar in nature to his action the previous December.

> [We should] express our indignation and concern at the proceedings in North America, and to assure the King that we will assist him in enforcing [all] the laws of this Kingdom.

The resolution effectively called for implementation of the Stamp Act, enforcement with military power. No one was misled by the mild words or the law he meant to enforce. Such a step calls for the use of armed force: sending troops to America. The motion led to heated debate, Grenville arguing that "whoever advises the King to give up his sovereignty over America is the greatest enemy to this country and will be accused by all posterity." Conway opposed the resolution.

> If we enforce the Stamp Act, we shall have a war in America, and the Bourbon league will take this advantage. [And therefore] a war with America would immediately be followed by a war with the continent.[14]

On February 10, Lord George Sackville explained the result of the motion by Grenville. It did not make sense to divide on the motion itself, since "we could not well give a direct negative to a proposition which, taken abstractedly, every body must approve of." A motion instead for the chairman to leave the chair was successful by a division of 274 to 134, a resounding defeat for Grenville.[15]

The defeat was so decisive that the Grenville faction abandoned any notion of retaining the act as it was, having hope only for modification rather than repeal.

Advocates for Repeal

In parallel with petitions from the port and manufacturing towns bemoaning the dire economic situation, the ministry brought forth a parade of advocates during the second week in February to give further evidence of the economic distress caused by the Stamp Act, distress that could be relieved only by repeal of the act.[16]

On February 11, Barlow Trecothick was called as the first witness. The bulk of his testimony had to do with the economic situation. Asked, "Is the trade in North America now stopped?" He was blunt: "Almost wholly." He explained that the colonies "have restricted not to be shipped unless the Stamp Act is repealed." As part of his statement that "no modification will satisfy them," he addressed the issue of taxation: "From their writings I collect they think the right of Imposing Taxes is confined to the Assemblies." He had a chance to qualify that broad statement (supporting the Rockingham strategy of avoiding the colonial wholesale denial of the authority of Parliament to tax the colonies).

> Q. Has not that objection [i.e., assemblies exclusive right to impose taxes] been made to external taxes?
> A. Only to the weight of taxes; none to the authority laying them.[17]

James West wrote Newcastle after the testimony on February 11, reporting that "Trecothick was examined four hours and gave a full clear and satisfactory account, of the distress at home and abroad and stated everything as he did to Your Grace this morning," an all but direct statement that the testimony had been rehearsed.[18]

James Harris, a follower of Grenville, saw widespread rehearsal of witnesses presented by the ministry.

> We examined witnesses, sitting each day till near ten o'clock—some of them were Americans, some Yorkshire manufacturers, and the leaders London merchants with Alderman Trecothick at their head, *all primed . . . to say everything against the Stamp Act,* and neither to answer nor to know anything on the other side.[19]

On February 13, William Reeve, a prominent Bristol merchant, testified that letters from America were making orders conditional on repeal. He starts that "the trade has suffered diminution lately."

> Q. To what extent?
> A. At present it is totally stagnated
> Q. Owing to what?
> A. To the confusion they are in on account of the Stamp Act
> Q. Have you any particular evidence of that?
> A. I have many letters that mention the cause of it. Reads a Letter from Boston of the 4th November last. Has 500 letters to the same purpose. That the Americans will not send orders unless act is repealed.[20]

Benjamin Franklin, whose fame made his words particularly authoritative, also gave testimony on February 13.[21] His testimony was a particularly important part of the strategy to avoid any hint that the colonies made a wholesale rejection of the authority of Parliament.

> Q. Was it an opinion in America before 1763, that the parliament had no right to lay taxes and duties there?
> A. I never heard any objection to the right of laying *duties to regulate commerce*; but a right to lay *internal* taxes was never supposed to be in parliament, as we are not represented there.
> Q. On what do you found your opinion, that the people in America made any such distinction?

The distinction being questioned is between, in Franklin's words, "duties to regulate commerce" and "internal taxes."

> A. I know that whenever the subject has occurred in conversation where I have been present, it has appeared to be the opinion of every one, that we could not be taxed in a parliament where we were not represented. But the payment of duties laid by act of parliament, as *regulations of commerce*, was never disputed.

The distinction he continued to draw was between the unacceptable right to tax the colonies, and the acceptable authority to impose duties in order to regulate commerce. He had not yet used the phrase "external taxes," but soon found it necessary to make an explicit comment about the internal/external distinction.

> Q. You say the Colonies have always submitted to external taxes, and object to the right of parliament only in laying internal taxes; now can you shew that there is any kind of difference between the two taxes to the Colony on which they may be laid?

He presented his definition of an external tax.[22]

> A. I think the difference is very great. An *external tax is a duty laid on commodities imported*; that duty is added to the first cost, and other charges on the commodity, and when it is offered to sale, makes a part of the price. If the people do not like it at that price, they refuse it; they are not obliged to pay it. But an internal tax is forced from the people without their consent, if not laid by their own representatives.

This established the idea that Americans believed a duty collected at an American port was an external tax. Franklin, perhaps carefully, intentionally, even deceptively, did not distinguish between duties laid for the regulation of trade and those for the purpose of raising revenue.

> Q. You say they [Americans] do not object to the right of parliament in laying duties on goods to be paid on their importation; now, is there any kind of difference between a duty on the importation of goods and an excise on their consumption?
> A. Yes, a very material one; an excise, for the reasons I just mentioned, they think you can have no right to lay within their country. But the sea is yours; you maintain, by your fleets, the safety of navigation in it, and keep it clear of pirates; *you may*

> *have therefore a natural and equitable right to some toll or duty* on merchandizes carried through that part of your dominions, towards defraying the expence you are at in ships to maintain the safety of that carriage.

Another question challenges him to justify the right to be taxed only with consent. He invoked "the common rights of Englishmen, as declared by Magna Charta, and the Petition of Right." That answer brought forth a question that could be difficult to handle.

> Q. Then may they not, by the same interpretation object to the parliament's right of external taxation?

Franklin gives this clever answer, evading the question but making an important point.

> A. They never have hitherto. Many arguments have been lately used here to shew them that there is no difference, and that if you have no right to tax them internally, *you have none to tax them externally*, or make any other law to bind them. At present they do not reason so, but in time they may possibly be convinced by these arguments.[23]

(The Americans will eventually reach this very conclusion.)

Franklin's performance was treated by contemporaries as being important, perhaps definitive, in leading to repeal of the Stamp Act. London printer William Strahan wrote David Hall, his friend and fellow printer in Philadelphia.

> Herewith I send you, what I promised in my last, Dr Franklin's Examination before the House of Commons . . . it is not very easy, in some Parts of it, to comprehend what many of the Questions lead to, or with what intent they were put.
>
> To this very Examination, more than to any thing else, you are indebted to the speedy and total Repeal of this odious Law. The Marquis of Rockingham told a Friend of mine a few Days

> after, That he never knew Truth make so great a Progress in so very short a Time. From that very Day, the Repeal was generally and absolutely determined, all that passed afterwards being only mere Form.[24]

On February 14, Henry Cruger Jr. wrote to his father in New York with this eyewitness summary.

> Tuesday the 11th Instant Mr. Trecothick was order'd to the Barr of the House of Commons. . . . [He was asked] if it was not his Opinion the Americans wou'd acquiesce with the Stamp Act provided it was mitigated? Mr. Trecothick answer'd, it was his Opinion, that no Modification of the Act wou'd reconcile it and that the Americans wou'd be contented with nothing less than a Total Repeal.

He explained the reaction to Trecothick's testimony.

> This inflamed Grenville's Party; they called you insolent Rebells. I dread his Party coming into Power before the Act is repeal'd. If they do, they'll certainly scourge you, altho some English Merchants are ruined by it.
>
> We have proved the Debt from the Continent of America, to England is five Millions Sterling. This Grenville attempted to disprove, and is what makes the Examinations at the Barr so tedious.

And summarized later events.

> All the principal Manufacturing Towns have sent Petitions for a Repeal of the Stamp Act. A Manufacturer from Leeds was order'd to the Barr, who said, since the Stagnation of the American Trade he has been constrained to turn off 300 Families out of 600 he constantly employ'd. . . . The Present Ministry see and have declared the Expediency of repealing on this ground.

> If the late Ministers come in again, and enforce the Act, they will have 20,000 unemployed Poor in a suppliant manner petitioning a Repeal of the S[tamp] Act, otherwise they must starve. So, I think there is no doubt but it must be repeal'd on some grounds, or some Cause or other, especially if you stick to your engagements of having no English Goods untill it is effectuated.

Cruger ventures a prediction.

> Today the Ministry wou'd have the best of it, and things wou'd look well; tomorrow Grenville and his Party wou'd gain the Power, and then of course no Repeal. The Vox Populi now begins to gain ground, and I think since the Legality of Taxation is allowed, the Act *will be repeal'd upon the Grounds of Expediency.*[25]

Decisions in the House of Commons

Garth summarized the discussions of February 10–13 and 17–18 in the committee of the House of Commons, working until "near Eleven each Night in proving the Allegations of the Petitions [treating with] the State of America before and since the Stamp Act. . . . This Enquiry finish'd in the Evening of the 18th. Mr. Conway gave Notice to the Committee that upon the 21st he shou'd move a Resolution [for the repeal of the Stamp Act]."[26] This was to be the seventh and final resolution to be considered.

Repeal Resolution in Committee

A much anticipated "great debate" on repeal occurred in the American Committee on February 21.[27] Conway begins the debate at "25 minutes before five," stressing "the extent of our trade to America . . . the distress of the manufacturers in this country."

> The principal trade of this country at an absolute stand. That if there ever was an Act which carried with it evil policy, it is the present, and carries oppression and impracticability in its very nature.

He pointed out the danger of enforcement: "The rebellion in America would be subdued, the force of this country is equal to it, but the conflict is death to both countries."

> Our forces in America are but about 5,000 men scattered over that immense continent. The men able to carry arms in America are great in number. Many of them have served in the American war. Many indeed of our own military forces are Americans and would be little disposed to fight against their countrymen. . . . If we were engaged in a civil war in America, a French and Spanish war would be the consequence, and this connected with an American war would be absolute ruin to this country.

Amendment is not the answer.

> No modification will satisfy them. They will look on it as a foundation for some future bold Ministry to build a tax which shall be the ruin of their property and their liberty at one and the same moment.

At the end of an almost hour-long speech he moved the repeal resolution.

> That the House be moved, that Leave be given to bring in a Bill to repeal an Act passed in the last session of Parliament, intitled [the title of the Stamp Act].

Charles Jenkinson was against repeal, but "sees the greatest difficulty on both sides of this question."

> If we do not repeal it, the disorder in America [and] the distress of our manufactures at home [will continue]. If we do repeal it, no minister will venture to tax them again. The Americans will never submit when they see resistance is the best argument for relief, and you will have the same argument urged not

> against this law alone but against every other which they do not perfectly approve of.

Jenkinson ended with an amendment to the question: "instead of repeal, to insert the words, explain and amend." It was understood that the result would be only a tax on small items; the purpose would be to demonstrate Parliament's right to levy a tax on the colonies.

In the very early morning of February 22, the amendment by Jenkinson was defeated and the resolution for repeal carried by a division of 275 to 167. There were more debates in the next few days, but this vote effectively decided the issue—at least for the House of Commons.

Seven Resolutions Approved

On February 24, seven resolutions were reported from the American Committee to the House of Commons. The declaratory resolution was the first; the repeal resolution was the seventh.

The first resolution passed after a short debate. The next five resolutions were approved with little discussion. The essence of those resolutions is:

> 2. That tumults and insurrections of the most dangerous nature have been raised, and carried on, in several of the North American colonies . . . in manifest violation of the laws and legislative authority of this kingdom.
> 3. That the said tumults and insurrections have been greatly countenanced and inflamed by votes and resolutions, passed in several of the assemblies . . . tending to destroy the legal and constitutional dependency of the said colonies on the Imperial crown and Parliament of Great Britain.
> 4. That such persons, who [assisted] in carrying into execution [acts of Parliament and] have suffered any injury or damage, ought to have full and ample compensation made to them.
> 5. [All such persons] . . . are therefore intitled to, and will assuredly have, the protection of the House of Commons of Great Britain.

> 6. That all persons who . . . have not been able to procure stamped paper . . . ought to be indemnified from all penalties and forfeitures, which they may have incurred, by [using paper] not duly stamped.[28]

A motion to recommit to the committee the repeal resolution generated a four-hour debate, ending with the motion being defeated 240 to 133.

Orders were given to bring in bills regarding the resolutions for the declaration of right, for indemnification, and for repeal (1, 6, 7). The other four resolutions were ordered to be "presented to His Majesty requesting they be transmitted to the colonial governors for them to be "communicated to the Assemblies" of each colony.[29] Resolution number four was intended to provide for compensation to British officials, such as Oliver and Hutchinson in Boston, who suffered property damage. The issue of compensation became a major source of controversy, primarily in Massachusetts.

Anticipating Repeal

On February 28, the committee of merchants of London trading to North America wrote their American counterparts, nominally "to acquaint you that a Bill is now in the House of Commons for repealing the Stamp Act" but with an agenda to advocate—almost demand—submissive conduct by the Americans. It was important that the Americans accepted the announced pretense for repeal.

> It had been a constant Argument against the Repeal, that in case it should take place, the Parliamentary Vote of Right will be waste paper, and that the Colonies will understand very well, that what is pretended to be adopted, on mere Commercial Principle of Expedience, is *really yielded thro' fear; and amounts to a tacit but effectual Surrender of its right* or at least a tacit Compact that it will never use it.

The committee explained that "the Act could certainly not have been repealed, had not Men's Minds been in some measure satisfied with the Declaration of Right." Finally,

> If [the repeal] is talked of as a Victory, if it is said the Parliament have yielded up the Right, then indeed your Enemies here will have a Complete Triumph. Your Friends must certainly lose all power to serve you. Your Tax Masters probably be restored.[30]

Many Americans were angry about the tone of the letter, and about similar admonitions from others that the Americans needed to show proper appreciation for the beneficence of Parliament. Prominent Virginian planter-politician George Mason, in his response of June 6 (eventually published in a London newspaper), made it clear that the repeal only corrected an error. The Americans "have been only contending for their birth-right, and have now only gained, or rather kept, what could not, with common justice, or even policy, be denied them." He also gave clear warning: "Such another experiment as the stamp act would produce a general revolt in America."[31]

By the end of February, the ministry felt the repeal was virtually assured (based on the large majority in preliminary votes, and the tradition that the Lords defer to the Commons regarding money bills). In order to calm the waters in America, Conway wrote to the governors on March 1 that although he could not give them any "positive Direction" about how to react "in the perplexed Situation of Things in the Colonies," it is his duty to explain that "a Bill is brought in, & has made some Progress, in the House of Commons, for the Repeal of the Stamp Act."[32]

Henry Cruger Jr. wrote on March 1 to Aaron Lopez: "The Stamp Act is not yet repeal'd, but it is as good as done." Those opposed to repeal "were only for a Modification of the Act." Cruger emphasized the method of reaching repeal, that Parliament first "settled their *Right* of taxing you," then "proceeded to the *Expediency* of repealing the Act, which never wou'd have come to pass had it not been for the Merchants and Manufacturers of England. Trade here was totally stagnated; not one [British merchant dealing with America] gave out a single order for goods on purpose to compel all manufacturers to engage with us in petitioning Parliament for a repeal of the Stamp Act. . . . I hugg myself the Parliament will never trouble America again."[33]

Richard Jackson wrote to Thomas Hutchinson on March 3.

> The Repeal is accompanied, as you have probably heard before, with another Bill declaring the Right of Parlt to make laws for binding the Colonies in all Cases whatsoever. I hope no ill Use will be made of this by alarming the People in America, believing as I do that our future Rule in America may be that we have used in Ireland.

He also explained that he had shared the manuscript of *A Brief State of the Claim of the Colonies.*

> I have intrusted Mr Conway, Secy of State, with a Copy of the MS piece you sent me last year. He knows indeed that you are the Author of it. This was a Piece of Confidence in him that I thought proper & have no reason to be sorry I reposed it. He has been a Principal Asistance to us in procuring the Repeal.[34]

Jackson also wrote to Governor Bernard on March 3, again dismissing the threat of the Declaratory Act.

> The stamp act is probably on the point of being repealed; since we have ventured to conclude that the House of Lords will hardly throw out the bill. *The repeal, however, could not have been obtained* without another act for declaring the right of Parliament to bind the colonies by laws in all cases whatsoever; which will probably as little prejudice them, as the power we claim in Ireland.[35]

Repeal

On March 4, the declaratory bill passed the House of Commons with little debate and no division. The same evening, after modest debate, the repeal bill passed on a division of 250 to 122, sending both bills to the House of Lords on March 5.[36]

In the House of Lords, the passage of the declaratory bill went smoothly. The repeal was turbulent, the lengthy debate being on

March 11 at the second reading of the bill. The result—for committing the bill—was close: 73–61.[37] The defeat of those opposed to repeal drew a dissent in ten parts that repeal would "make the Authority of Great Britain contemptible hereafter." Many of the individual statements, and certainly the overall tone of the dissent, turned out to be predictive of events and attitudes of the next decade.

> 7thly, Because the Reason assigned in the publick Resolutions of the Provincial Assemblies, in the North American Colonies, for their disobeying the Stamp Act, *videlicet*, "That they are not represented in the Parliament of Great Britain," extends to all other Laws, of what Nature soever, which that Parliament has enacted, or shall enact, to bind them in Times to come; and must (if admitted) set them absolutely free from any Obedience to the Power of the British Legislature.

The opinion of the colonists that "they have a Right to every Freedom of Trade which the Subjects of Great Britain now enjoy" is particularly egregious.

> [It] strikes directly at the Act of Navigation, and other subsequent Laws, which, from Time to Time, have been made on the wise Policy of that Act. And, should they ever be encouraged to procure for themselves that absolute Freedom of Trade which they appear to desire, our Plantations would become not only of no Benefit, but in the highest Degree prejudicial to the Commerce and Welfare of their Mother Country.

The ninth objection was that Americans would not believe the rationale given for repeal, rather that the insurrections accomplished "the very Point at which they aimed: the immediate Repeal of the Stamp Act without any previous Submission on the Part of the Colonies." In discussion of the Declaratory Act, they asserted that Parliament had "grievously injured its own Dignity and Authority by verbally asserting that Right which it substantially yields up to their Opposition."

> The Reasons assigned for this Concession render it still more alarming, as they arise from an illegal and hostile Combination of the People in America to distress and starve our Manufacturers, and to with-hold from our Merchants the Payment of their just Debts.[38]

On March 17, the repeal bill passed with little debate and without a division.[39] Following this final defeat, there was another written dissent, beginning with disparaging the declaration of right.

> The Declaratory Bill we passed last week cannot possibly obviate the growing Mischiefs in America, where it may seem calculated only to deceive the People of Great Britain, by holding forth a delusive and nugatory Affirmance of the Legislative Right of this Kingdom.

After three more statements the ending was dramatic.

> Lastly, Because the Repeal of this Law, under the present Circumstances, will, we fear, not only surrender the Honour and essential Interests of the Kingdom, now and for ever, both at Home and Abroad, but will also deeply affect the fundamental Principles of our Constitution.[40]

Resulting Acts of Parliament

The declaratory and repeal acts received the royal assent on March 18.

Declaratory Act (6 George III c. 12). The title:

> An act for the better securing the dependency of his Majesty's dominions in America upon the crown and parliament of Great Britain.

The preamble. First, the need for the act, based on illegal claims of the colonies.

> Whereas several of the houses of representatives in His Majesty's colonies and plantations in America have of late, against law, claimed to themselves, or to the general assemblies of the same, the sole and exclusive right of imposing duties and taxes [and have] . . . passed certain votes, resolutions, and orders derogatory to the legislative authority of Parliament, and inconsistent with the dependency of the said colonies and plantations upon the crown of Great Britain:

The declaration.

> may it therefore . . . be declared . . . That the said colonies and plantations in America have been, are, and of right ought to be, subordinate unto, and dependent upon the imperial crown and parliament of Great Britain;
>
> and that the King's majesty, by and with the advice and consent of the lords spiritual and temporal, and commons of Great Britain, in parliament assembled, had, hath, and of right ought to have, full power and authority to make laws and statutes of sufficient force and validity to bind the colonies and people of America, subjects of the crown of Great Britain, in all cases whatsoever.

The second clause, that pronouncements of the colonies denying the authority of Parliament were null and void, had little effect on future actions.

An Act Repealing the Stamp Act (6 George III c. 11). The title:

> An act to repeal an act made in the last session of parliament, intituled [states the title of the Stamp Act].

The preamble (the only section of the act).

> Whereas an act was passed in the last session of parliament intitled [the Stamp Act] and whereas the continuance of the said

> act *would be attended with many inconveniencies, and may be productive of consequences greatly detrimental to the commercial interests of these kingdoms.* . . . That from and after [May 1, 1766] the above-mentioned act, and the several matters and things therein contained, shall be, and is and are hereby repealed and made void to all intents and purposes whatsoever.

Indemnity Act (6 George III c. 51): it received the royal assent on June 6. The title alone states the essence of the act.

> An Act for indemnifying Persons who have incurred certain Penalties, inflicted by an Act of the last Session of Parliament, for granting certain Stamp Duties, in the British Colonies and Plantations in America; and for making valid all instruments executed or inrolled there on unstamped paper, vellum, or parchment.

There had been some minor controversy in the House of Commons over whether or not there should be a requirement for retroactive payment of duties on the use of unstamped paper, but the bill was finally passed with no such requirement.[41]

The formal notification of the Declaratory Act and the repeal of the Stamp Act came in the form of a circular letter of March 31 from Secretary of State Conway. He warned

> that the least Coolness, or Unthankfulness, the least Murmuring or Dissatisfaction on any Ground whatever of former heat, or too much prevailing Prejudice, may fatally endanger that Union, & give the most severe and affecting Blow to the future Interests of both Countries.

The repeal was based on "the Moderation, the Forbearance, the unexampled Lenity, and Tenderness of Parliament towards the Colonies." He warned that "the future Happiness and Prosperity of the Colonies" will depend upon their "chearful Obedience to the Laws and legislative Authority of Great Britain" and demonstration of "respectful Gratitude to the mother Country."[42] Such "obedience" was to be to the laws as understood by the British—including taxation so long as it was imposed upon trade, not as internal taxes.

ANTI-SEJANUS, writing in the *London Chronicle* in February 1766 while repeal was not yet settled, indicated that he understood the situation and foresaw what was likely to occur. He wrote that the current disposition of the Americans

> is owing in a great measure to the inconveniences under which they are laid by the Act of Navigation; and they seem determined, at all events, to rid themselves of it. The opposition which they make to the Stamp-act is only the beginning of troubles.

A repeal of the act will not satisfy the Americans.

> They might indeed for a few months lay down their arms, but they would still be working underhand, and collecting strength daily; till at last the seditious flame would burst out afresh, and having been for a-while pent up, would rage afterwards with redoubled fury.
>
> The Americans imbibe notions of independance and liberty with their very milk, and will some time or other shake off all subjection. If we yield to them in this particular, by repealing the Stamp-Act, it is all over; they will from that moment assert their freedom.[43]

Anti-Sejanus was correct in his final statement regarding assertion of their freedom. David Ramsay, a contemporary historian of the American Revolution, wrote in 1789 the following.

> The repeal of the stamp act . . . was the first direct step to American independency. The claims of the two countries were not only left undecided, but a foundation was laid for their ex-

tending at a future period, to the impossibility of a compromise.[44]

Twelve

Aftermath

"There was no one action of his life that he could blame himself for, but his changing his ministers in 1765, and consenting to the repeal of the Stamp Act. . . . Could he have foreseen the consequences, he certainly would not have passed the Act, but it was to the repeal he imputed all the subsequent misfortunes."

—King George III, June 1779

THE AMERICANS DID NOT see the repeal of the Stamp Act in 1766 as being the result of the "Moderation, the Forbearance, the unexampled Lenity, and Tenderness of Parliament." In fact, they saw repeal as having been forced by their resistance—ending with the capitulation of Parliament. Accordingly, the colonists demonstrated no "chearful Obedience to the Laws and legislative Authority of Great Britain." The American responses were polite, showing respectful gratitude, but no colony admitted to a right in Parliament to tax the colonies.

TRIUMPHANT COLONIALS

Repeal had been achieved by specific actions: first, preventing the act from coming into effect by mob action, intimidation, and violence when necessary, and second, causing widespread economic distress in Great Britain, thereby gaining political leverage in Parliament. "Men who had influence over the people considered the repeal as a victory. An experiment had been made, which persuaded them that by union and firmness, the colonies would be able to carry every point they wished for."[1] Dickinson had written Pitt in December 1765 that repeal would "be regarded as the Correction" of an error by the previous ministry. True enough, but the Americans also held "that Great Britain by repealing that act will tacitly acknowledge that she has no Right to tax the Colonies."

The American attitude appeared even before any formal notification of the repeal (rumors of repeal being widespread). At a Boston town meeting of April 21, 1766, "the Honourable James Otis Esq. was chosen Moderator." The purpose of the meeting was "to agree on such Measures of Conduct as may be proper when we shall receive certain advice of the Repeal of the Stamp Act." The resulting plan was to praise British leaders for "a happy Repeal of the Stamp Act" but at the same time to assert that the repeal was simply righting a wrong: "so unconstitutional as well as grievous to his Majesty's good Subjects of America," and that the repeal returns "our incontestable Right of Internal Taxation."[2] Governor Bernard reported this speech by the moderator.

> [Otis] told the People that *the distinction between inland taxes & port duties was without foundation*; for whoever had a right to impose one had a right to impose the other: & therefore as the Parliament had given up the one (for, he said, the Act for securing the dependency had no relation to taxes) they had given up the other; & the Merchants were great fools, if they submitted any longer to the Laws restraining their Trade, which ought to be free.[3]

Bernard feared "that the ravings of this Man will be taken for the Sentiments of the Americans."[4]

Confirmation of the repeal soon arrived.

> On the 16th of May, a copy of the act of parliament for the repeal of the stamp act was brought to Boston. No rejoicings, since the revolution, had been equal to those on this occasion. The general language from the friends of liberty to such as had differed from them, was this: "See what firmness and resolution will do." . . . The act which accompanied [the repeal], with the title of, "securing the dependency of the colonies," caused no allay of the joy, and was considered as mere naked form.
>
> The scent of victory was in the air.
>
> The repeal of the stamp act, notwithstanding the declaratory act which accompanied it, was considered throughout the colonies not as a mere act of favour . . . but as a concession, made to the claim of exemption from taxes while not represented.[5]

It did not take long for the British to learn about the reaction in America. After hearing from his friend Robert Nugent that "repeal of the Stamp Act . . . produced universal joy" in America, Grenville responded on June 21 that repeal would establish a precedent.

> I have not the least doubt that our brethren in America will express great joy at the repeal of the Stamp Act, especially if they understand by it, as they justly may, notwithstanding the Declaratory Bill passed at the same time, that they are thereby exempted for ever from being taxed by Great Britain for the public support even of themselves.[6]

Sugar Act of 1766

In June, Parliament passed a modification to the Sugar Act that repealed the threepence duty on foreign molasses and replaced it by a duty of one penny per gallon on all molasses, British as well as foreign. This change (the singular action taken to resolve colonial commercial grievances) transformed the duty into a tax, no longer having any connection with regulation of trade. Americans celebrated the reduction in the molasses duty as being a favorable British response to their complaints about the previous excessive duty, paying the one penny with only rare and scattered complaints (the duty typically not being recognized as a tax). Such American acceptance of an external tax reinforced the position advanced by the Rockingham ministry that external taxation was acceptable to the Americans.[7]

Change in Government

The Rockingham ministry fell (for complicated political reasons having little to do with the situation in America) shortly after the Stamp Act was repealed, replaced by one led by William Pitt. Rockingham was insistent on claiming his ministry had been a success (even that "the Repeal of the Stamp Act had had all the good effect that could be proposed").[8] However, his claim was disputed.

British subminister William Knox (previously an agent for Georgia, now chief pamphleteer for the Grenville faction) claimed that Rockingham had misled Parliament as to the cause of the depressed economy, and to its correction. It was "given in evidence to parliament, in March 1766" that the Stamp Act caused the drop in orders from the colonies. Further, it was claimed that "should the stamp-act be repealed, trade would again flourish." Such a happy circumstance never came to pass.

> The stamp-act was repealed, and every other American proposition adopted; and, from the Custom-house entries, it now appears, that the exports to the North American colonies in the year 1766, instead of being double the value, as was promised, actually fell short of the exports in 1765.[9]

Townshend Revenue Act

The dismissal of Rockingham brought about a change more important than the change in first minister. Charles Townshend, appointed chancellor of the exchequer, came to have a powerful influence on the taxation decisions of the government. He revealed his attitude toward taxing the colonies as part of a discussion on January 26, 1767, in the House of Commons. Connecticut agent William Samuel

Johnson described the event when he wrote to Governor William Pitkin on February 12.

> Mr. Townsend, Chancellor of the Exchequer, a few days past, upon an accidental mention of America, said in the House, "I do not know any distinction between internal and external taxes; it is a distinction without a difference, it is perfect nonsense; *if we have a right to impose one, we have the other.*"[10]

Townshend mentioned the issue again on February 18, saying that "the distinction between internal and external taxes [is] not founded in reason but proper to be adopted in policy."[11]

On May 13, Townshend declared that he planned

> to lay taxes upon America, but not internal taxes, because though he did not acknowledge the distinction it was accepted by many Americans and this was sufficient.[12]

Johnson, writing on May 16, provided more insight into Townshend's viewpoint.

> Although he did not in the least doubt the right of Parliament to tax the Colonies internally, and that he knew no difference between internal and external taxes (which, by the way, is a doctrine very generally adopted here), yet since the Americans were pleased to make that distinction he was willing to indulge them, and chose for that reason to *confine himself to regulations of trade, by which a sufficient revenue might be raised in America.*[13]

The resulting Townshend Revenue Act, an "Act for granting certain duties in the British colonies and plantations in America" received the royal assent on June 29, 1767. Its purpose was straightforward: "Whereas it is expedient that a revenue should be raised in your Majesty's dominions in America."[14] The duties act was one of the Townshend Acts of 1767 that advanced the new imperial policy begun in 1763. Duties were laid on goods imported from Great Britain (including tea), to be paid at American ports. They appeared to exactly fit the definition of external taxes that were acceptable to Americans (particularly as stated by Benjamin Franklin).

To the surprise of the British (despite ample warning from colonial resolutions and petitions), Americans saw the Townshend duties as unconstitutional taxes, equivalent to internal taxes, and resisted, just as they had the Stamp Act, with protests, petitions, and nonimportation. It is not too much to say that this became the "Townshend Duties Crisis." Lieutenant Governor Hutchinson was not surprised. Almost three years previously, he observed that if duties were "for the sake of the money arising from the Duties" then, asking rhetorically, "how are the privileges of the people less affected than by an internal tax," meaning that such duties *were identical in effect* as internal taxes.

Troubled Future

On March 4, 1768, Governor Bernard wrote to Secretary at War Lord Barrington about a colonial response to the Townshend duties.

> The Traders here are now associating in the *same Manner that they did at the Time of the Stamp Act.* . . . When they are asked what will satisfy them, the Answer is a total Repeal of the Laws of Trade imposing Duties and nothing less. And untill such Repeal shall be made they propose to suspend the Execution of the Laws, as they did in the Stampt Act, which is now made a Precedent. However there has not as yet been a violent Opposition to the Officers; but it is hourly expected.[15]

On April 16, Barrington responded to Bernard.

> I see with Grief, but not with surprize, the open attempts towards independency making in New England & I conclude the other northern Colonies. A man must have been blind who did not foresee that consequence, from the repeal of the Stamp Act.[16]

By late 1768, British dismay about American resistance was widespread. During a debate on November 8, Barrington gave a long account of the disturbances in America, ending with identification of the beginning of the troubles—and his opinion of the Americans.

> He wished the Stamp act had never been passed. He called the Americans traitors, worse than traitors, against the Crown—traitors against the legislature of this country.[17]

The next five years were increasingly turbulent with the repeal being cited as a continuing problem. Following the Boston Tea Party of December 1773 the king acknowledged the consequences.

> All men seem now to feel that the fatal compliance in 1766 has encouraged the Americans annually to encrease in their pretensions [to independence] . . . which is quite subversive of the obedience which a Colony owes to its Mother Country.[18]

In 1774, in the House of Commons, during a debate on April 19 that centered around a proposition to repeal the tax on tea imposed by the Townshend Acts (the other import duties having been repealed in 1770), one speaker made explicit the fact that the Americans had taken advantage of each British concession to advance to further demands.

> In 1765 they resisted the Stamp Act, but acquiesced to the Act of 1764, imposing external taxation. It was thought the repeal of the Stamp Act would quiet and satisfy the Americans. It was repealed, but the consequence did not appear, for they then urged that we did it because we knew we had no right to tax them at all. That is what they now contend for and have dropped the idea of internal and external. If we repeal this, they will next say we have no power in any case to make laws to bind them.[19]

Affairs went downhill from there. In 1779, the colonies, having declared their independence and Great Britian at war with America and her new ally France, King George III gathered his principal ministers to meet with him. He expressed his feelings about the events of 1765 and 1766.

> There was no one action of his life that he could blame himself for, but his changing his ministers in 1765, and consenting to the repeal of the Stamp Act. . . . Could he have foreseen the consequences, he certainly would not have passed the Act, but it was to the repeal he imputed all the subsequent misfortunes.[20]

NOTES

PREFACE

1. Joseph J. Ellis, *The Cause: The American Revolution and Its Discontents, 1773–1783* (Liveright, 2021), 7. I provide a foundation for the three acts in *1764: The First Year of the American Revolution* (Westholme Publishing, 2021), and deal with the first act in *The Sugar Act and the American Revolution* (Westholme Publishing, 2023).

2. This right was stated in October 1765 as the consensus opinion of the colonies.

3. Merrill Jensen, *The Founding of a Nation: A History of the American Revolution, 1763–1775* (Oxford University Press, 1968), 153. See also Edmund S. Morgan and Helen M. Morgan, *The Stamp Act Crisis: Prologue to Revolution*, third edition (University of North Carolina Press, 1995), first published in 1953 by University of North Carolina Press, and P. D. G. Thomas, *British Politics and the Stamp Act Crisis: The First Phase of the American Revolution, 1763–1767* (Clarendon Press, 1975).

4. Commentary by Merrill Jensen in Randolph G. Adams, *Political Ideas of the American Revolution*, third edition (Barnes & Noble, 1958), 19, first published in 1922 by Trinity College; P. D. G. Thomas, *Revolution in America: Britain and the Colonies, 1763*–1776 (University of Wales Press, 1992), 15.

5. Charles Francis Adams, ed., *The Works of John Adams, Second President of the United* States, vol. 10 (Little, Brown, 1856), 180. A letter to Thomas McKean, November 26, 1815.

PROLOGUE

1. It received the royal assent on April 25, 1694. Unless otherwise cited, this prologue is based on H. Dagnall, *Creating a Good Impression: Three Hundred Years of the Stamp Office and Stamp Duties* (His Majesty's Stationary Office, 1994), 3–12.

2. Edward Hughes, "The English Stamp Duties, 1664–1764," *English Historical Review* 56, no. 222 (1941): 234–64 (quotation 245).

CHAPTER ONE: REVENUE

1. Jensen, *Founding of a Nation*, 71; George Bancroft, *History of the United States, from the Discovery of the American Continent*, vol. 5 (Little, Brown, 1852), 88n–89n.

2. The broader problem was what the British perceived as the "inconstancy of the American colonists." It led to the need for a change in colonial policy, "a

complete overhaul of the colonial system." Thomas C. Barrow, *Trade and Empire: The British Customs Service in Colonial America, 1660–1775* (Harvard University Press, 1967), 173. I deal with the perceived problem of inconstancy of the colonists in *The Sugar Act and the American Revolution.* (It was not simply a sugar problem of course, but the Sugar Act "was far more comprehensive than its popular name implied." Jensen, *Founding of a Nation*, 47.)

3. William James Smith, ed., *The Grenville papers: being the correspondence of Richard Grenville, earl Temple, K.G., and the right Hon: George Grenville, their friends and contemporaries*, vol. 2 (John Murray, 1852), 374, hereafter, *Grenville papers*. See also John L. Bullion, *A Great and Necessary Measure: George Grenville and the Genesis of the Stamp Act* (University of Missouri Press, 1982), and Charles R. Ritcheson, "The Preparation of the Stamp Act," *The William and Mary Quarterly* 10, no. 4 (1953): 543–59.

4. James Munro, ed., *Acts of the Privy Council of England: Colonial Series,* vol. 4. A.D. 1745–1766 (His Majesty's Stationary Office, 1911), 569–72. For background to the report, and more detail on Grenville's legislation, see Thomas C. Barrow, "Background to the Grenville Program, 1757–1763," *The William and Mary Quarterly* 22, no. 1 (1965): 93–104.

5. George Reese, ed., *The Official Papers of Francis Fauquier Lieutenant Governor of Virginia, 1758–1768,* vol. 2. 1761–1763, Virginia Historical Society Documents, vol. 15 (University Press of Virginia, 1981), 993–94.

6. Colin Nicolson, ed., *The Papers of Francis Bernard: Governor of Colonial Massachusetts, 1760–1769*, vol. 1: 1759–1763, The Colonial Society of Massachusetts, vol. 73 (The Society, 2007), 381–82. This letter arrived in Boston on September 14.

7. Ibid., 432.

8. Colin Nicolson, ed., *The Papers of Francis Bernard: Governor of Colonial Massachusetts, 1760–1769*, vol. 2: 1764–1765, Colonial Society of Massachusetts, vol. 81 (The Society, 2012), 29.

9. Merril Jensen, ed., *Tracts of the American Revolution, 1763–1776* (Bobbs-Merrill, 1966, 3–18.

10. John Russell Bartlett, ed., *Records of the Colony of Rhode Island and Providence Plantations, in New England*, vol. 6, 1757–1769 (General Assembly, 1861), 378–83.

11. Leonard W. Labaree, ed., *The Papers of Benjamin Franklin,* vol. 10 (Yale University Press, 1966), 415.

12. Leonard W. Labaree, ed., *The Papers of Benjamin Franklin*, vol. 11 (Yale University Press, 1967), 35. A letter of January 26, 1764.

13. Great Britain. Parliament, *The Parliamentary History of England, From the Earliest Period to the Year 1803*, vol. 15. A. D. 1753–1765 (T. C. Hansard, 1813), 1337, 1340–41, hereafter, *Parliamentary History.*

14. All quotations of March 9–10 are from R. C. Simmons and P. D. G. Thomas, eds., *Proceedings and Debates of the British Parliaments Respecting North America, 1754–1783*, vol. 1, 1754–1764 (Kraus International, 1982), 487–95, hereafter, *Proceedings and Debates.*

15. See Edmund S. Morgan, "The Postponement of the Stamp Act," *The William and Mary Quarterly* 7, no. 3 (1950): 353–92.
16. Massachusetts Historical Society, *Jasper Mauduit: Agent in London for the Province of the Massachusetts-Bay 1762–1765*, Massachusetts Historical Society Collections, vol. 74 (The Society, 1918), 159n, hereafter, *Jasper Mauduit: Agent in London.*
17. Ibid., 147n.
18. Virginia Historical Society, "Virginia Legislative Documents (continued)," *The Virginia Magazine of History and Biography*, vol. 10, no. 1 (July 1902): 1–16 (quotation, 3–4).
19. Todd Andrlik, *Reporting the Revolutionary War: Before it was History, it was News* (Sourcebooks, 2012), 4–5.
20. *Proceedings and Debates*, 1:492–95; Danby Pickering, *The Statutes at Large, from Magna Charta to the end of the Eleventh Parliament of Great Britain, Anno 1761*, vol. 26 (Printed by Joseph Bentham, 1764), 33–52.
21. Such courts are thoroughly discussed in Carl Ubbelohde, *The Vice-Admiralty Courts and the American Revolution* (University of North Carolina Press, 1960).
22. Pickering, *Statutes at Large*, 26:103–05.
23. *Jasper Mauduit: Agent in London*, 147n. Jasper was reporting secondhand from his brother Israel, who attended the meeting.
24. Franklin B. Dexter, ed., "A Selection from the Correspondence and Miscellaneous Papers of Jared Ingersoll," *Papers of the New Haven Colony Historical Society*, vol. 9 (The Society, 1918), 201–472 (quotation, 293–95). Hereafter, *Ingersoll Papers.*
25. Ibid., 298–300.
26. Connecticut Historical Society, *The Fitch Papers,* vol. 2: January 1759–May 1766, Collections of the Connecticut Historical Society, vol. 18 (The Society, 1920), 289, hereafter, *Fitch Papers.*
27.Massachusetts Historical Society, *The Bowdoin and Temple Papers*, Massachusetts Historical Society, sixth ser., vol. 9 (The Society, 1897), 22–26, hereafter, *Bowdoin and Temple Papers.*
28. Jack M. Sosin, *Agents and Merchants: British Colonial Policy and the Origins of the American Revolution, 1763–1775* (University of Nebraska Press, 1965), 54n; Franklin B. Wickwire, *British Subministers and Colonial America, 1763–1783* (Princeton University Press, 1966), 105–10.
29. Hughes, "English Stamp Duties," 259.
30. Nicolson, ed., *Papers of Francis Bernard*, 2:87.
31. Ibid., 2:471–79.
32. Edward Channing and Archibald Coolidge, eds., *The Barrington-Bernard Correspondence* (Harvard University, 1912), 81.
33. Nicolson, ed., *Papers of Francis Bernard*, 2:98–99.
34. John W. Tyler and Elizabeth Dubrulle, eds., *The Correspondence of Thomas Hutchinson,* vol. 1: 1740–1766, Colonial Society of Massachusetts, vol. 84 (The Society, 2014), 208–17. Its date is stated as "11-23 July 1763."
35. Ibid., 1:207.

CHAPTER TWO: PROTEST

1. Bernard Bailyn, ed., *Pamphlets of the American Revolution, 1750–1776*, vol. 1, 1750–1765 (Harvard University Press, 1965), 300–354. Bailyn points out that "the constitutional issue he had exposed . . . lay at the heart of the Anglo-American struggle" (299).
2. Ibid., 1:319–23.
3. Jack P. Greene, *The Constitutional Origins of the American Revolution* (Cambridge University Press, 2011), 82. Greene sees the internal/external problem as one of how "to allocate authority in such a way as to preserve the British rights of colonists in the distant polities in America while providing a measure of central direction for the empire as a whole." He discusses other contemporary essayists (80–86, 187).
4. New York. General Assembly, *Journal of the Votes and Proceedings of the General Assembly of the Colony of New-York. Began the 8th Day of November, 1743; and Ended the 23d of December, 1765,* vol. 2 (Published by Order of the General Assembly, 1766), 749–50, hereafter, *General Assembly of the Colony of New-York.*
5. New York Historical Society, *The Colden Letter Books,* vol. 1. 1760–1765, Collections of the New York Historical Society, vol. 9 (Printed for the Society, 1877), 361.
6. *General Assembly of the Colony of New-York*, 2:776–79.
7. Charles J. Hoadly, *The Public Records of the Colony of Connecticut* [1636-1776], vol. 12 (General Assembly, 1881), 256, 651–71.
8. Ibid., 12:653, 657–61, 671. See also Lawrence Henry Gipson, *The Coming of the Revolution, 1763–1775* (Harper, 1954), 76–77.
9. Tyler and Dubrulle, eds., *Correspondence of Thomas Hutchinson,* 1:237–38.
10. City of Boston. Registry Department, *A Report of the Record Commissioners of the City of Boston, Containing the Boston Town Records, 1758 to 1769*, vol. 16 (Rockwell and Churchill, 1886), 121–22, hereafter, *Report of the Record Commissioners.*
11. Massachusetts. General Court. House of Representatives, *Journals of the House of Representatives of Massachusetts:* 1764–1765, vol. 41 (Massachusetts Historical Society, 1971), 72–77.
12. Bailyn, ed., *Pamphlets*, 1:474–82.
13. Ibid., 1:474–76.
14. Bailyn, ed., *Pamphlets*, 1:418–82. Bailyn discusses problems with writings by Otis, ending with, "By 1776 Otis' argument . . . was blatantly self-contradictory." Bernard Bailyn, *The Ideological Origins of the American Revolution* (Harvard University Press, 2017, originally published 1967), 204-07.
15. *Fitch Papers*, 2:284–85.
16. Nicolson, ed., *Papers of Francis Bernard*, 2:90.
17. Proceedings of the Massachusetts Historical Society, "The Thatcher Papers," Proceedings of the Massachusetts Historical Society, vol. 20 (The Society, 1884), 49–52.
18. Alden Bradford, ed., *Speeches of the Governors of Massachusetts from 1765 to 1775* (Russell and Gardner, 1818), 21–23.

19. *Jasper Mauduit: Agent in London*, 170–71.
20. Nicolson, ed., *Papers of Francis Bernard*, 2:263.
21. Tyler and Dubrulle, eds., *Correspondence of Thomas Hutchinson*, 1:239–40.
22. Bartlett, ed., *Records of the Colony of Rhode Island*, 6:415–16.
23. Ibid., 6:416–27. Bernard Bailyn, in *Ideological Origins*, 1:210–13, discusses the relationship between Bland, Fitch, and Hopkins in terms of internal and external spheres of government.
24. Bartlett, ed., *Records of the Colony of Rhode Island*, 6:416, 420, 422–26.
25. John Pendleton Kennedy, ed., *Journals of the House of Burgesses of Virginia, 1761–1765* (Library Board of the State of Virginia, 1907), 256–57.
26. Kennedy, ed., *Journals of the House of Burgesses*, 302–04.
27. George Reese, ed., *The Official Papers of Francis Fauquier Lieutenant Governor of Virginia, 1758–1768*, vol. 3: 1764–1768, Virginia Historical Society Documents, vol. 16 (University Press of Virginia, 1983), 1201–02.
28. R. W. Gibbes, *Documentary History of the American Revolution, 1764–1776* (D. Appleton, 1855), 2.
29. Bernhard Knollenberg, *Origin of the American Revolution: 1759–1766* (Macmillan, 1960), 214.
30. Charles F. Hoban, ed., *Votes and Proceedings of the House of Representatives of the Province of Pennsylvania*, Pennsylvania Archives, eighth ser, vol. 7 (Bureau of Publications, 1935), 5644.
31. William L. Saunders, ed., *The Colonial Records of North Carolina,* vol. 6: 1759–1765 (Joseph Daniels, 1888), 1261.

CHAPTER THREE: BACKLASH

1. Jensen, *Founding of a Nation*, 62.
2. Andrlik, *Reporting the Revolutionary War*, 7.
3. E. B. O'Callaghan, ed., *Documents relative to the colonial history of the State of New-York; procured in Holland, England, and France*, vol. 7 (New York State Legislature, 1856), 678. See also Lawrence Henry Gipson, *The British Empire before the American Revolution*, vol. 10, *The Triumphant Empire: Thunder-Clouds Gather in the West, 1763–1766* (Knopf, 1961), 274n.
4. Munro, ed., *Acts of the Privy Council of England: Colonial Series*,. 4:692.
5. Gordon S. Wood, ed., *The American Revolution: Writings from the Pamphlet Debate 1764–1772,* vol. 1 (The Library of America, 2015), 165–240.
6. Ibid., 231, 233–34, 236, 237.
7. L. B. Namier, "Charles Garth, Agent for South Carolina: Part II (Continued)," *English Historical Review* 54, no. 216 (1939), 632–52 (quotation, 648–49).
8. *Jasper Mauduit: Agent in London*, 168n–69n.
9. Namier, "Charles Garth," 649.
10. *Ingersoll Papers*, 312–14.
11. *Bowdoin and Temple Papers*, 37.
12. Neil R. Stout, ed., "The Missing Temple-Whately Papers," *Proceedings of the Massachusetts Historical Society,* third ser, vol. 104 (1992), 123–47 (quotation 135). A letter of February 9 to Temple.

13. Great Britain. Historical Manuscripts Commission, *Tenth Report of The Royal Commission on Historical Manuscripts* (Eyre and Spottiswoode, 1885), 382. Hereafter, *Tenth Report of The Royal Commission on Historical Manuscripts.*

CHAPTER FOUR: THE STAMP ACT

1. *Ingersoll Papers*, 306–08.
2. The approved resolutions are given in full at R. C. Simmons and P. D. G. Thomas, eds., *Proceedings and Debates of the British Parliaments Respecting North America, 1754–1764*, vol. 2, *1765–1768* (Kraus International, 1983), 17–24.
3. The following discussion in the House of Commons, unless otherwise indicated, is from *Proceedings and Debates*, 2:8–17. See also Thomas, *British Politics*, 88–100.
4. *Ingersoll Papers*, 310–11. His phrase "Sons of Liberty," using it in a generic manner for all men who were fierce advocates of freedom, was adopted by Americans to name a militant resistance group.
5. *Bowdoin and Temple Papers*, 49.
6. Namier, "Charles Garth," 649–50.
7. *Proceedings and Debates*, 2:25–27.
8. Namier, "Charles Garth," 650–51, writing on February 17.
9. *Ingersoll Papers*, 316–17.
10. *Bowdoin and Temple papers*, 61, to Temple.
11. Wickwire, *British Subministers*, 190–91.
12. *Proceedings and Debates*, 2:29–31; Great Britain. House of Commons, *Journals of the House of Commons*, vol. 30 (His Majesty's Stationary Office, 1803), 192–93, 293; Thomas, *British Politics*, 97–98.
13. The following extracts from the act are from Pickering, *Statutes at Large*, 26:179–204.
14. *Ingersoll Papers*, 338.
15. *Bowdoin and Temple papers*, 51.

CHAPTER FIVE: DENIAL

1. Jensen, *Founding of a Nation*, 100, 107–08. Andrlik, *Reporting the Revolutionary War*, 10.
2. The resolves of all nine assemblies (Virginia, Rhode Island, Pennsylvania, Maryland, Connecticut, Massachusetts, South Carolina, New Jersey, and New York) can be found in Morgan, ed., *Prologue to Revolution*, 47–62. See also Edmund S. Morgan, "Colonial Ideas of Parliamentary Power 1764–1766," *The William and Mary Quarterly* 5, no. 3 (1948), 311–41.
3. Reese, ed., *Papers of Francis Fauquier*, 3:1250.
4. Kennedy, ed., *Journals of the House of Burgesses*, 360.
5. Ibid., lxvi–lxvii. The newspaper was quoted in the 1907 introduction to the journal of the Burgesses. An editorial comment asserted that Patrick Henry was behind the release of all the resolutions and the previously unpublished pream-

ble. When Henry found it impossible to have all the resolutions passed by the Burgesses, "it was determined that they should be printed for the benefit of the Colonies," ibid., lxvi.

6. Nicolson, ed., *Papers of Francis Bernard*, 2:295–96, 301; C. E. Carter, ed., *The Correspondence of General Thomas Gage with the Secretaries of State*, vol. 1 (Yale University Press, 1931), 67. Writing on September 23.

7. Reese, ed., *Papers of Francis Fauquier*, 3:1314–17.

8. Bradford, ed., *Speeches of the Governors of Massachusetts*, 34–35.

9. Thomas Hutchinson, *The History of the Province of Massachusetts Bay: from 1749 to 1774*, vol. 3 (John Murray, 1828), 118.

10. Bradford, ed., *Speeches of the Governors of Massachusetts*, 36.

11. Nicolson, ed., *Papers of Francis Bernard*, 2:285–87.

12. Bradford, ed., *Speeches of the Governors of Massachusetts*, 39–40.

13. Nicolson, ed., *Papers of Francis Bernard*, 2:367–69.

14. Bradford, ed., *Speeches of the Governors of Massachusetts*, 45.

15. Bartlett, ed., *Records of the Colony of Rhode Island*, 6:450–52.

16. Morgan, ed., *Prologue to Revolution*, 51–52.

17. Leonard W. Labaree, ed., *The Papers of Benjamin Franklin*, vol. 12 (Yale University Press, 1968), 207–08, 279–80.

18. Bailyn, ed., *Pamphlets*, 1:607–58. Bailyn notes that the pamphlet "played a significant role in the debate in Parliament on the repeal of the Stamp Act" (599).

19. Bailyn, ed., *Pamphlets*, 1:610–12, 615–16, 619–20, 637–38, 652.

20. Morgan, ed., *Prologue to Revolution*, 118–22.

CHAPTER SIX: STAMP ACT CONGRESS

1. Supreme Court justice Joseph Story made an insightful account of the Stamp Act Congress. "§190. Perhaps the best general summary of the rights and liberties asserted by all the colonies is contained in the celebrated declaration drawn up by the Congress of the Nine Colonies assembled at New York, in October 1765." Joseph Story, *Commentaries on the Constitution of the United States*, vol. 1 (Hilliard, Gray, and Company, 1833), 133.

2. New York Historical Society, *The Colden Letter Books*, vol. 2. 1765–1775, Collections of the New York Historical Society, vol. 10 (Printed for the Society, 1878), 35. Hereafter, *Colden Letter Books*.

3. Carter, ed., *Correspondence of General Thomas Gage*, 1:69–70.

4. Stamp Act Congress, *Proceedings of the Congress at New York* (Printed by Jonas Green, 1766). All the following quotations of formal products of the congress are from this source. See also Clinton Alfred Weslager, *The Stamp Act Congress: With an Exact Copy of the Complete Journal* (University of Delaware Press, 1976).

5. Joseph Story quotes the statement, phrasing it this way, that "§191. . . there is 'a material distinction in reason and sound policy between the necessary exercise of parliamentary jurisdiction in general acts . . . and the exercise of that jurisdiction by imposing taxes on the colonies;' thus admitting the former to be rightful, while denying the latter." Story, *Commentaries*, 1:134.

6. Timothy Pitkin, *A Political and Civil History of the United States of America, from the year 1763 to the Close of the Administration of President Washington*, vol. 1 (Hezekiah Howe, 1828), 448–54.
7. Weslager, *Stamp Act Congress*, 224–30.
8. *Fitch Papers*, 2:366–67.
9. Hoadly, *Public Records of the Colony of Connecticut*, 12:423–24.
10. Bradford, ed., *Speeches of the Governors of Massachusetts*, 50–51. The date of October 25 is incorrect.
11. *General Assembly of the Colony of New-York*, 2:800.
12. Ibid., 2:807–08.

CHAPTER SEVEN: NONIMPORTATION

1. A detailed analysis of hard times in the colonies and the reaction to the duties of the Stamp Act is provided by Arthur M. Schlesinger, *The Colonial Merchants and the American Revolution, 1763–1766* (Columbia University, 1918). Schlesinger especially made the point that although there were many problems having to do with "the collapse of the artificial war-time prosperity which the provinces had enjoyed, . . . the chief cause of the hard times was the restrictive legislation of 1764." Ibid., 56–57. See also Charles M. Andrews, "The Boston Merchants and the Non-importation Movement," Publications of the Colonial Society of Massachusetts: *Transactions, 1916–1917*, vol. 19 (The Society, 1918), 159–259.
2. Historical Society of Pennsylvania. "Extracts from the Letter-Book of Samuel Rhoads, Jr.," *Pennsylvania Magazine of History and Biography*, vol. 14 (The Society, 1890), 423.
3. William Allen and Lewis Burd Walker, *Extracts from Chief Justice William Allen's Letter Book* (Standard Publishing Company, 1897), 65–66.
4. Abram English Brown, *John Hancock: His Book* (Lee and Shepard, 1898), 61–64, 69, 83, 87–88, 90.
5. Gipson, *Coming of the Revolution*, 106.
6. Agreements to not import British goods derived "their importance less as economic measures than as political protests." In fact, "the adoption of non-importation agreements added no new difficulty to the situation already existing." Schlesinger, *Colonial Merchants*, 80–81.
7. Merrill Jensen, ed., *English Historical Documents, American Colonial Documents to 1776*, vol. 9 (Eyre & Spottiswoode, 1955), 671–72.
8. Carter, ed., *Correspondence of General Thomas Gage*, 1:73.
9. Jedidiah Morse, *Annals of the American Revolution: Or, A Record of the Causes And Events Which Produced, And Terminated In the Establishment And Independence of the American Republic* (Jedidiah Morse, 1824), 127–28.
10. Labaree, ed., *Papers of Benjamin Franklin*, 12:388–89.
11. Brown, *John Hancock*, 103–04.
12. *Colden Letter Books*, 2:77–78. For how British public opinion affected matters, see Dora M. Clark, *British Opinion and the American Revolution* (Yale University Press, 1930).

13. Colin Nicolson, ed., *The Papers of Francis Bernard: Governor of Colonial Massachusetts, 1760–1769*, vol. 4: 1768, Colonial Society of Massachusetts, vol. 86 (Colonial Society of Massachusetts, 2015), 135–36.

CHAPTER EIGHT: NULLIFICATION

1. Nicolson, ed., *Papers of Francis Bernard*, 2:295–96.
2. Ibid., 2:301–05.
3. Ibid., 2:321. To Jackson, August 24.
4. Ibid., 2:422, 424n4. To John Pownall, November 26.
5. Tyler and Dubrulle, eds., *Correspondence of Thomas Hutchinson*, 1:406. He wrote this in a draft letter dated March 8, 1766; a letter never sent but that shows his understanding of the situation.
6. Nicolson, ed., *Papers of Francis Bernard*, 2:308.
7. Ibid., 2:315–17. Bernard spins story after remorseful story about the difficulties he faces. His comments were not without influence and often quoted in the reports of the Privy Council.
8. Ibid., 2:338–40.
9. Ibid., 2:323.
10. Ibid., 2:367–70.
11. Ibid., 2:391, 396.
12. Ibid., 2:397–98.
13. Ibid., 2:413–15. *Supreme Imperial Legislature* is a loaded phrase. A widely accepted doctrine of the time was that in every sovereign state there must be a single, uncontestable supreme authority. Historian Gordon Wood puts it in the spotlight: "This was the most important concept of eighteenth-century English political theory, and it became the issue over which the empire was finally broken." Gordon S. Wood, *The American Revolution: A History* (Modern Library, 2002), 43.
14. Nicolson, ed., *Papers of Francis Bernard*, 2:428, 429n. For the role of the newspapers in fostering nullification, see Arthur M. Schlesinger, *Prelude to Independence, the Newspaper War on Britain, 1764–1776* (Knopf, 1958).
15. Nicolson, ed., *Papers of Francis Bernard*, 2:361.
16. Ibid., 2:376.
17. Ibid., 2:447.
18. The riot is described in detail in Massachusetts Historical Society, "Stamp Act Riot in Newport," *Proceedings of the Massachusetts Historical Society*, vol. 55 (The Society, 1923), 234–37.
19. Bartlett, ed., *Records of the Colony of Rhode Island*, 6:453–57.
20. Ibid., 478–79. Other governors had a similar reaction. Connecticut Governor Fitch responded in December that "there is no Distributor of Stamps here nor any Stamps Received that I know of in the Colony." *Fitch Papers*, 2:381–82.
21. O'Callaghan, ed., *Documents*, 7:761.
22. *Colden Letter Books*, 2:27.
23. Ibid., 2:30.
24. Ibid., 2:35–37.

25. Carter, ed., *Correspondence of General Thomas Gage*, 1:67–68.
26. G. D. Scull, ed., *The Montresor Journals*, Collections of the New York Historical Society for the Year 1881, vol. 14 (The Society, 1882), 336.
27. O'Callaghan, ed., *Documents*, 7:770.
28. *Colden Letter Books*, 2:54–56.
29. Carter, ed., *Correspondence of General Thomas Gage*, 1:70–71.
30. Ibid., 1:73.
31. Ibid., 1:78–79.
32. The most thorough description of the organization is provided by historian Pauline Maier. She emphasizes that despite some peripheral violence, the Sons of Liberty were part of American "ordered resistance," demonstrating devotion to "the basic fabric of established government." Pauline Maier, *From Resistance to Revolution: Colonial Radicals and the Development of American Opposition to Britain, 1765–1776* (W. W. Norton, 1972), 76, 112.
33. William Gordon, *The History of the Rise, Progress, and Establishment of the Independence of the United States of America,* vol. 1 (Printed for the Author, 1788), 186–87.
34. Cadwallader Colden, *The Letters and Papers of Cadwallader Colden,* vol. 7 (1765–1775), in New York Historical Society Collections, vol. 56 (Printed for the Society, 1923), 94–95.
35. Jensen, ed., *English Historical Documents*, 9:670–71.
36. Nicolson, ed., *Papers of Francis Bernard*, 3:67, 69.
37. Gordon, *History of the Rise*, 195–98. Boston was not represented but was later sent a copy of the agreement.
38. Labaree, ed., *Papers of Benjamin Franklin*, 12:261. To Benjamin Franklin.
39. Morgan and Morgan, *Stamp Act Crisis*, 161.
40. Labaree, ed., *Papers of Benjamin Franklin*, 12:264.
41. Samuel Hazard, ed., *The Register of Pennsylvania: Devoted to the Preservation of Facts and Documents and Every Other Kind of Useful Information Respecting the State of Pennsylvania*, vol. 2 (W. F. Geddes, 1828), 247.
42. *Ingersoll Papers*, 341–46, 347, 354.
43. Labaree, ed., *Papers of Benjamin Franklin*, 12:278; Scull, ed., *Montresor Journals*, 340.
44. Reese, ed., *Papers of Francis Fauquier*, 3:1290–94, 1297.
45. Jensen, ed., *English Historical Documents*, 9:680–82.
46. Gipson, *British Empire*, 10:317.
47. Ibid., 10:322.
48. Maier, *From Resistance to Revolution*, 93–94.
49. Labaree, ed., *Papers of Benjamin Franklin*, 12:376–77.
50. Nicolson, ed., *Papers of Francis Bernard*, 2:437, 440.
51. Ibid., 2:438.
52. Ibid., 2:442–43.
53. Colin Nicolson, ed., *The Papers of Francis Bernard: Governor of Colonial Massachusetts, 1760–1769*, vol. 3: 1766–1767, Colonial Society of Massachusetts, vol. 83 (The Society, 2013), 59.

54. Ibid., 3:71, 77, 79, 98–99.

CHAPTER NINE: REACTION

1. Smith, ed., *Grenville papers*, 3:215–16.
2. Thomas, *British Politics*, 11–13, 85, 120–21.
3. Sir John Fortescue, ed., *Correspondence of King George the Third from 1760 to December 1783*, vol. 1 (Macmillan, 1927), 347. A letter of May 28, 1766. The principal historian of the ministry is Paul Langford, *The First Rockingham Administration: 1765–1766* (Oxford University Press, 1973).
4. Gertrude S. Kimball, ed., *The Correspondence of the Colonial Governors of Rhode Island 1723–1775*, vol. 2 (Houghton, Mifflin, 1903), 367.
5. "To go against the Great Commoner's desires, Rockingham felt, would be fatal." Charles R. Ritcheson, *British Politics and the American Revolution* (University of Oklahoma Press, 1954), 52.
6. John Almon, *A Collection of Interesting, Authentic Papers, Relative to the Dispute between Great Britain and America . . . from 1764 to 1775* (Printed for John Almon, 1777), 38.
7. Reese, ed., *Papers of Francis Fauquier*, 3:1275–76.
8. Almon, *Collection of Interesting . . .*, 9.
9. Great Britain. Parliament, *The Parliamentary History of England, From the Earliest Period to the Year 1803,* vol. 16. A. D. 1765–1771 (T.C. Hansard, 1813), 121–22.
10. Ibid., 16:123.
11. *Bowdoin and Temple Papers*, 72.
12. Smith, ed., *Grenville papers*, 3:100.
13. Munro, ed., *Acts of the Privy Council of England: Colonial Series*, 4:732–33.
14. Ibid., 4:733.
15. *Parliamentary History*, 16:116–18. This is a generic version of the letter sent to all governors.
16. Nicolson, ed., *Papers of Francis Bernard*, 2:385–87.
17. John L. Bullion, "British Ministers and American Resistance to the Stamp Act," October–December 1765. *The William and Mary Quarterly* 49, no. 1 (1992), 89–107, especially 98–99.
18. Tyler and Dubrulle, eds., *Correspondence of Thomas Hutchinson*, 1:447.
19. Smith, ed., *Grenville papers*, 3:107.
20. *Parliamentary History*, 16:119.
21. *Colden Letter Books*, 2:95.
22. James Munro, ed., *Acts of the Privy Council of England: Colonial Series. "The Unbound Papers,"* vol. 6. (His Majesty's Stationary Office, 1912), 412–15.

CHAPTER 10: DECISION

1. Fred J. Hinkhouse, *The Preliminaries of the American Revolution as Seen in the English Press, 1763–1775* (Columbia University Press, 1926), 44.
2. Ibid., 55–56.

3. Walter E. Minchinton, "The Stamp Act Crisis: Bristol and Virginia," *Virginia Magazine of History and Biography* 73, no. 2 (1965), 145–55.
4. Brown, *John Hancock*, 69.
5. Hinkhouse, *Preliminaries of the American Revolution*, 44; Massachusetts Historical Society, *Commerce of Rhode Island, [1726–1800]*, vol. 1, 1726–1774, Collections of the Massachusetts Historical Society, seventh ser., vol. 9 (The Society, 1914), 123, 125. Hereafter, *Commerce of Rhode Island*; Hinkhouse, *Preliminaries of the American Revolution*, 62; Minchinton, "Stamp Act Crisis," 147, 151.
6. Minchinton, "Stamp Act Crisis," 152–53.
7. Labaree, ed., *Papers of Benjamin Franklin*, 12:362–65.
8. Bradford, ed., *Speeches of the Governors of Massachusetts*, 69–70.
9. *Fitch Papers*, 2:376.
10. Langford, *First Rockingham Administration*, 111.
11. Lord John Russell, *Correspondence of John, Fourth Duke of Bedford*, vol. 3 (Longman, Brown, et al, 1846), 323. A letter of November 28.
12. Lucy S. Sutherland, "Edmund Burke and the First Rockingham Ministry," *English Historical Review* 47, no. 185 (1932), 46–72 (quotation, 62n).
13. Morgan, ed., *Prologue to Revolution*, 129.
14. *Proceedings and Debates*, 2:192.
15. Albert Matthews, ed., *Letters of Dennys De Berdt 1757–1770* (Colonial Society of Massachusetts, 1911), 307–08.
16. *Proceedings and Debates*, 2:54–60.
17. *Tenth Report of The Royal Commission on Historical Manuscripts*, 399.
18. Langford, *First Rockingham Administration*, 131–32. See also Thomas, *British Politics*, 160–64 and Gipson, *British Empire*, 10:375–76.
19. *Fitch Papers*, 2:383–84.
20. Hinkhouse, *Preliminaries of the American Revolution*, 72.
21. *Proceedings and Debates*, 2:63–64, 73.
22. The following discussion, unless otherwise indicated, is based on *Proceedings and Debates*, 2:84–91.
23. *Proceedings and Debates*, 2:91. P. D. G. Thomas asserted that the report by West "is more accurate than one published [earlier] on which many historians have relied." *Revolution in America*, 68. In other writing, Thomas noted additional contemporary sources (e.g., Burke, Franklin, Garth) that support the idea that Pitt denied "Parliament's right to levy *internal* taxation." He goes so far as to assert that "the weight of evidence makes it essential to correct the contention of [Morgan and Morgan, *Stamp Act Crisis*, 283–85] that Pitt did not distinguish between internal and external taxation." Thomas, *British Politics*, 172n.
24. Matthews, ed., *Dennys De Berdt*, 310.
25. Joseph W. Barnwell, "Hon. Charles Garth, M.P., the Last Colonial Agent of South Carolina in England, and Some of His Work," *The South Carolina Historical and Genealogical Magazine*, 26, no. 2 (1925), 67–92 (quotation, 71). This is from a long letter dated January 19, 1766, but written over a number of days with subsections for January 30 and February 9.

26. Lilian Dickins and Mary Stanton, eds., *An Eighteenth-century Correspondence* (John Murray, 1910), 431.
27. Langford, *First Rockingham Administration*, 143.
28. The resolutions as agreed, with modifications proposed by Yorke on January 24, are at Earl of Albemarle, ed., *Memoirs of the Marquis of Rockingham and His Contemporaries: With original letters and documents now first published*, vol. 1 (Richard Bentley, 1852), 285–87.
29. Albemarle, ed., *Memoirs of the Marquis of Rockingham*, 1:287.
30. Matthews, ed., *Dennys De Berdt*, 311–12. The date of the meeting was not provided by De Berdt in the letter of February 15.

CHAPTER ELEVEN: REPEAL OF THE STAMP ACT
1. *Proceedings and Debates*, 2:95–96.
2. Barnwell, "Hon. Charles Garth," 73; *Proceedings and Debates*, 2:104.
3. Barnwell, "Hon. Charles Garth," 74–75; *Proceedings and Debates*, 2:109–13.
4. Fortescue, ed., *Correspondence of King George*, 1:246.
5. Matthews, ed., *Dennys De Berdt*, 312.
6. Barnwell, "Hon. Charles Garth," 76.
7. *Proceedings and Debates*, 2:121. January 31.
8. Ibid., 2:293. There are multiple versions of the declaratory resolution. For simplicity, this is the version debated and approved in the House of Commons on February 3.
9. Unless otherwise indicated, the quoted material of the debates on February 3 is from *Proceedings and Debates*, 2:135–45.
10. Barnwell, "Hon. Charles Garth," 84–85.
11. *Proceedings and Debates*, 2:124.
12. William T. Laprade, "The Stamp Act in British Politics." *American Historical Review* 35, no. 4 (1930), 735–57 (quotation, 752).
13. *Proceedings and Debates*, 2:151–66.
14. Ibid., 2:167–73.
15. *Proceedings and Debates*, 2:175; Great Britain. Historical Manuscripts Commission, *Report on the Manuscripts of Mrs. Stopford-Sackville*, vol. 1 (His Majesty's Stationary Office, 1904), 107.
16. The lengthy testimony is addressed in *Proceedings and Debates*, 2:185–276.
17. Ibid., 2:185–94.
18. Ibid., 2:185.
19. Ibid., 2:218.
20. Ibid., 2:221.
21. Franklin's testimony is from *The Examination of Doctor Benjamin Franklin, Before an August Assembly, Relating to the Repeal of the Stamp-Act, &c.*, in Wood, ed., *Writings from the Pamphlet Debate*, 1:333–61. Gordon Wood was unequivocal in his assessment of the importance of this testimony. The Rockingham ministry called upon Franklin "to provide cover for Parliament's repeal of the Stamp Act." Ibid., 1:332.

22. Bernard Bailyn asserts that at this point in the controversy the internal-external "distinction became crucial" because "it allowed him to evade the question of whether or not his countrymen were in principle denying Parliament's right to tax them." Franklin was "forced to defend it." When asked, "Did he really believe that such a distinction was valid? Yes, Franklin assured them, he did; the difference between 'external' and 'internal' taxing was 'very great.'" Bailyn, *Ideological Origins*, 214.
23. Wood, ed., *Writings from the Pamphlet Debate*, 1:341, 343, 348, 359.
24. William Strahan, "Correspondence between William Strahan and David Hall, 1763–1777 (Continued)." *Pennsylvania Magazine of History and Biography* 10, no. 2 (1886), 217–32 (quotation, 220-21). Letter of May 10.
25. *Commerce of Rhode Island*, 1:139-43.
26. Barnwell, "Hon. Charles Garth," 90; *Proceedings and Debates*, 2:263–77.
27. Unless otherwise indicated, the following is from *Proceedings and Debates*, 2:280–89. See also Lawrence Henry Gipson, "The Great Debate in the Committee of the Whole House of Commons on the Stamp Act, *Pennsylvania Magazine of History and Biography* 86, no. 1 (1962), 10–41.
28. The resolutions are given in full at *Proceedings and Debates*, 2:293–95.
29. Ibid., 2:296–302.
30. Proceedings of the Massachusetts Historical Society, "London Merchants on the Stamp Act Repeal," Proceedings of the Massachusetts Historical Society, third ser., vol. 11 (The Society, 1923), 215–23 (quotations, 216–17).
31. Morgan, *Prologue to Revolution*, 159, 162.
32. *Fitch Papers*, 2:391–92.
33. *Commerce of Rhode Island*, 1:145–46.
34. Tyler and Dubrulle, eds., *Correspondence of Thomas Hutchinson*, 1:400.
35. Bradford, ed., *Speeches of the Governors of Massachusetts*, 72.
36. *Proceedings and Debates*, 2:310–17.
37. Ibid., 2:335–46.
38. Ibid., 2:331–34.
39. Ibid., 2:354.
40. Ibid., 2:351–53.
41. Danby Pickering, *The Statutes at Large, from Magna Charta to the end of the Eleventh Parliament of Great Britain, Anno 1761*, vol. 27 (John Archdeacon, 1767), 19–20, 273–74.
42. Nicolson, ed., *Papers of Francis Bernard*, 3:134–36.
43. Morgan, ed., *Prologue to Revolution*, 134.
44. David Ramsay, *The History of the American Revolution*, vol. 1 (R. Aitken and Son, 1789), 74.

CHAPTER TWELVE: AFTERMATH

1. Hutchinson, *History of the Province*, 3:148.
2. *Report of the Record Commissioners*, 16:175.
3. Nicolson, ed., *Papers of Francis Bernard*, 3:279–80. Writing much later to the secretary of state on December 22.

4. Ibid., 3: 146. To Jackson on April 28.
5. Hutchinson, *History of the Province*, 3:147, 167.
6. Smith, ed., *Grenville papers*, 3:248–50.
7. "If the colonists had been more intent on their theoretical rights than on immediate business concessions, the keener minds would have perceived that rejoicing was premature." It was a tax. "It was an unvarnished contradiction of the colonial claim to 'no taxation without representation.'" Schlesinger, *Colonial Merchants*, 85.
8. Mary Bateson, ed., *A Narrative of the Changes in the Ministry 1765–1767* (Longmans, Green, 1898), 79. Described by the Duke of Newcastle in a letter of July 11, 1766.
9. William Knox, *The Present State of the Nation: Particularly with Respect to its Trade, Finances, etc. etc.*, third edition (J. Almon, 1768), 41.
10. Massachusetts Historical Society, "The Trumbull Papers," *Collections of the Massachusetts Historical Society*, 5th ser., vol. 9 (The Society, 1885), 215–16. Hereafter, "Trumbull Papers."
11. *Proceedings and Debates*, 2:428–29.
12. *Proceedings and Debates*, 2:464.
13. "Trumbull Papers," 229.
14. Pickering, *Statutes at Large*, 27:503–12 (quotations, 503).
15. Nicolson, ed., *Papers of Francis Bernard*, 4:108.
16. Ibid., 4: 144–45.
17. R. C. Simmons and P. D. G. Thomas, eds., *Proceedings and Debates of the British Parliaments Respecting North America, 1754–1783*, vol. 3, 1768–1773 (Kraus International, 1984), 9.
18. Sir John Fortescue, ed., *The Correspondence of King George the Third from 1760 to December 1783*, vol. 3 (Macmillan, 1928), 59. A note of February 4, 1774.
19. R. C. Simmons and P. D. G. Thomas, eds., *Proceedings and Debates of the British Parliaments Respecting North America, 1754–1783*, vol. 4, Jan-May 1774 (Kraus International, 1985), 229.
20. Great Britain. Royal Commission on Historical Manuscripts, *Report on Manuscripts in Various Collections*, vol. 6 (His Majesty's Stationary Office, 1909), 260. A comment on June 21, related by Lord George Germain to William Knox.

BIBLIOGRAPHY

Adams, Charles Francis, ed. *The Works of John Adams, Second President of the United* States, vol. 10. Boston: Little, Brown, 1856.

Adams, Randolph G. *Political Ideas of the American Revolution*, third edition. New York: Barnes & Noble, 1958, first published 1922.

Albemarle, Earl of, ed. *Memoirs of the Marquis of Rockingham and His Contemporaries: With original letters and documents now first published*, vol. 1. London: Richard Bentley, 1852.

Allen, William and Lewis Burd Walker. *Extracts from Chief Justice William Allen's Letter Book*. Pottsville, PA: Standard Publishing Company, 1897.

Almon, John. *A Collection of Interesting, Authentic Papers, Relative to the Dispute between Great Britain and America . . . from 1764 to 1775*. London: printed for John Almon, 1777.

Andrews, Charles M. "The Boston Merchants and the Non-importation Movement," Publications of the Colonial Society of Massachusetts: *Transactions, 1916-1917*, vol. 19. Boston: The Society, 1918.

Andrlik, Todd. *Reporting the Revolutionary War: Before it was History, it was News*. Naperville, IL: Sourcebooks, 2012.

Bailyn, Bernard, ed. *Pamphlets of the American Revolution, 1750–1776*, vol. 1, 1750-1765. Cambridge, MA: Harvard University Press, 1965.

Bailyn, Bernard. *The Ideological Origins of the American Revolution*. Cambridge, MA: Harvard University Press, 2017, originally published 1967.

Bancroft, George. *History of the United States, from the Discovery of the American Continent*, vol. 5. Boston: Little, Brown, 1852.

Barnwell, Joseph W. "Hon. Charles Garth, M.P., the Last Colonial Agent of South Carolina in England, and Some of His Work," *The South Carolina Historical and Genealogical Magazine*, 26, no. 2. 1925.

Barrow, Thomas C. "Background to the Grenville Program, 1757-1763," *WMQ* 22, no. 1. 1965.

———. *Trade and Empire: The British Customs Service in Colonial America, 1660-1775*. Cambridge, MA: Harvard University Press, 1967.

Bartlett, John Russell, ed. *Records of the Colony of Rhode Island and Providence Plantations, in New England*, vol. 6, 1757-1769. Providence: General Assembly, 1861.

Bateson, Mary, ed. *A Narrative of the Changes in the Ministry 1765-1767*. London: Longmans, Green, 1898.

Bradford, Alden, ed. *Speeches of the Governors of Massachusetts from 1765 to 1775*. Boston: Russell and Gardner, 1818.

Brown, Abram English. *John Hancock: His Book*. Boston: Lee and Shepard, 1898.

Bullion, John L. *A Great and Necessary Measure: George Grenville and the Genesis of the Stamp Act*. Columbia: University of Missouri Press, 1982.

———. "British Ministers and American Resistance to the Stamp Act," October-December 1765. *WMQ* 49, no. 1. 1992.

Carter, C. E., ed. *The Correspondence of General Thomas Gage with the Secretaries of State*, vol. 1. New Haven, CT: Yale University Press, 1931.

Channing, Edward and Archibald Coolidge, eds. *The Barrington-Bernard Correspondence*. Cambridge, MA: Harvard University, 1912.

City of Boston. Registry Department, *A Report of the Record Commissioners of the City of Boston, Containing the Boston Town Records, 1758 to 1769*, vol. 16. Boston: Rockwell and Churchill, 1886.

Clark, Bullion John L. Bullion, A Great and Necessary Measure: George Grenville and the Genesis of the Stamp Act. Columbia: University of Missouri Press, 1982.

Dora M. *British Opinion and the American Revolution.* New Haven, CT: Yale University Press, 1930.

Colden, Cadwallader. *The Letters and Papers of Cadwallader Colden,* vol. 7. 1765-1775, in NYHS Collections, vol. 56. New York: Printed for the Society, 1923.

Connecticut Historical Society. *The Fitch Papers,* vol. 2: January 1759-May 1766, Collections of the Connecticut Historical Society, vol. 18. Hartford: The Society, 1920.

Dagnall, H. *Creating a Good Impression: Three Hundred Years of the Stamp Office and Stamp Duties.* London: His Majesty's Stationary Office, 1994.

Dexter, Franklin B. ed. "A Selection from the Correspondence and Miscellaneous Papers of Jared Ingersoll," *Papers of the New Haven Colony Historical Society*, vol. 9. New Haven, CT: The Society, 1918.

Dickins, Lilian and Mary Stanton, eds. *An Eighteenth-century Correspondence.* London: John Murray, 1910.

Ellis, Joseph J. *The Cause: The American Revolution and Its Discontents, 1773-1783.* New York: Liveright, 2021.

Fortescue, Sir John, ed. *Correspondence of King George the Third from 1760 to December 1783*, vol. 1. London: Macmillan, 1927.

——. *The Correspondence of King George the Third from 1760 to December 1783*, vol. 3. London: Macmillan, 1928.

Gibbes, R. W. *Documentary History of the American Revolution, 1764-1776.* New York: D. Appleton, 1855.

Gipson, Lawrence Henry. *The Coming of the Revolution, 1763-1775.* New York: Harper, 1954.

——. *The British Empire before the American Revolution*, vol. 10, *The Triumphant Empire: Thunder-Clouds Gather in the West, 1763–1766.* New York: Knopf, 1961.

——. "The Great Debate in the Committee of the Whole House of Commons on the Stamp Act," *PMHB* 86, no. 1. 1962.

Gordon, William. *The History of the Rise, Progress, and Establishment of the Independence of the United States of America,* vol. 1. London: Printed for the Author, 1788.

Great Britain. Historical Manuscripts Commission. *Tenth Report of*

The Royal Commission on Historical Manuscripts. London: Eyre and Spottiswoode, 1885.

——. *Report on the Manuscripts of Mrs. Stopford-Sackville*, vol. 1. London: HMSO, 1904.

Great Britain. House of Commons. *Journals of the House of Commons*, vol. 30. London: HMSO, 1803.

Great Britain. Parliament. *The Parliamentary History of England, From the Earliest Period to the Year 1803*, vol. 15. A. D. 1753-1765. London: T. C. Hansard, 1813.

——. *The Parliamentary History of England, From the Earliest Period to the Year 1803*, vol. 16. A. D. 1765–1771. London: T.C. Hansard, 1813.

Great Britain. Royal Commission on Historical Manuscripts. *Report on Manuscripts in Various Collections*, vol. 6. Dublin: HMSO, 1909.

Greene, Jack P. *The Constitutional Origins of the American Revolution*. New York: Cambridge University Press, 2011.

Hazard, Samuel, ed. *The Register of Pennsylvania: Devoted to the Preservation of Facts and Documents and Every Other Kind of Useful Information Respecting the State of Pennsylvania*, vol. 2. Philadelphia: W. F. Geddes, 1828.

Hinkhouse, Fred J. *The Preliminaries of the American Revolution as Seen in the English Press, 1763-1775*. New York: Columbia University Press, 1926.

Historical Society of Pennsylvania. "Extracts from the Letter-Book of Samuel Rhoads, Jr.," *Pennsylvania Magazine of History and Biography. PMHB*, vol. 14. Philadelphia: The Society, 1890.

Hoadly, Charles J. *The Public Records of the Colony of Connecticut* [1636-1776], vol. 12. Hartford: General Assembly, 1881.

Hoban, Charles F., ed. *Votes and Proceedings of the House of Representatives of the Province of Pennsylvania,* Pennsylvania Archives, eighth ser. vol. 7. Philadelphia: Bureau of Publications, 1935.

Hughes, Edward. "The English Stamp Duties, 1664-1764," *English Historical Review*. 56, no. 222. 1941.

Hutchinson, Thomas. *The History of the Province of Massachusetts Bay: from 1749 to 1774*, vol. 3. London: John Murray, 1828.

Jensen, Merrill, ed. *English Historical Documents. EHD, American Colonial Documents to 1776*, vol. 9. London: Eyre & Spottiswoode, 1955.

———. *Tracts of the American Revolution, 1763-1776*. Indianapolis, IN: Bobbs-Merrill, 1966.

———. *The Founding of a Nation: A History of the American Revolution, 1763-1775*. New York: Oxford University Press, 1968.

Kennedy, John Pendleton, ed. *Journals of the House of Burgesses of Virginia, 1761–1765*. Richmond: Library Board of the State of Virginia, 1907.

Kimball, Gertrude S., ed. *The Correspondence of the Colonial Governors of Rhode Island 1723-1775*, vol. 2. New York: Houghton, Mifflin, 1903.

Knollenberg, Bernhard. *Origin of the American Revolution: 1759–1766*. New York: Macmillan, 1960.

Knox, William. *The Present State of the Nation: Particularly with Respect to its Trade, Finances, etc. etc.*, third edition. London: J. Almon, 1768.

Labaree, Leonard W., ed. *The Papers of Benjamin Franklin,* vol. 10. New Haven, CT: Yale University Press, 1966.

———. *The Papers of Benjamin Franklin,* vol. 11. New Haven, CT: Yale University Press, 1967.

———. *The Papers of Benjamin Franklin,* vol. 12. New Haven, CT: Yale University Press, 1968.

Langford, Paul. *The First Rockingham Administration: 1765-1766*. London: Oxford University Press, 1973.

Laprade, William T. "The Stamp Act in British Politics," *American Historical Review* 35, no. 4. 1930.

Maier, Pauline. *From Resistance to Revolution: Colonial Radicals and the Development of American Opposition to Britain, 1765–1776*. New York: W. W. Norton, 1972.

Massachusetts General Court. House of Representatives. *Journals of the House of Representatives of Massachusetts:* 1764-1765, vol. 41. Boston: Massachusetts Historical Society, 1971.

Massachusetts Historical Society. "The Bowdoin and Temple Papers," *Collections of the Massachusetts Historical Society*, sixth ser., vol. 9. Boston: The Society, 1897.

——. *Commerce of Rhode Island [1726-1800]*, vol. 1, 1726-1774, Massachusetts Historical Society, seventh ser., vol. 9. Boston: The Society, 1914.

——. *Jasper Mauduit: Agent in London for the Province of the Massachusetts-Bay 1762–1765*, Massachusetts Historical Society, vol. 74. Boston: The Society, 1918.

——. "London Merchants on the Stamp Act Repeal," *Proceedings of the Massachusetts Historical Society*, third ser., vol. 11. Boston: The Society, 1923.

——. "Stamp Act Riot in Newport," *Proceedings of the Massachusetts Historical Society*, vol. 55. Boston: The Society, 1923.

——. "The Thatcher Papers," *Proceedings of the Massachusetts Historical Society*, vol. 20. Boston: The Society, 1884.

——. "The Trumbull Papers," *Collections of the Massachusetts Historical Society*, 5th ser., vol. 9. Boston: The Society, 1885.

Matthews, Albert, ed. *Letters of Dennys De Berdt 1757-1770*. Cambridge: Colonial Society of Massachusetts, 1911.

Minchinton, Walter E. "The Stamp Act Crisis: Bristol and Virginia," *VMHB* 73, no. 2. 1965.

Morgan, Edmund S. "Colonial Ideas of Parliamentary Power 1764-1766," *WMQ* 5, no. 3. 1948.

——. "The Postponement of the Stamp Act," *WMQ* 7, no. 3. 1950.

Morgan, Edmund S. and Helen M. Morgan. *The Stamp Act Crisis: Prologue to Revolution*, third edition. Chapel Hill: University of North Carolina Press, 1995, first published 1953.

Morse, Jedidiah. *Annals of the American Revolution: Or, A Record of the Causes And Events Which Produced, And Terminated In the Establishment And Independence of the American Republic.* Hartford, CT: Jedidiah Morse, 1824.

Munro, James, ed. *Acts of the Privy Council of England: Colonial Series. APC.* vol. 4. A.D. 1745–1766. London: HMSO, 1911.

——. *Acts of the Privy Council of England: Colonial Series. "The Unbound Papers,"* vol. 6. London: HMSO, 1912.

Namier, L. B. "Charles Garth, Agent for South Carolina: Part II. Continued," *EHR* 54, no. 216. 1939.

New York. General Assembly, *Journal of the Votes and Proceedings of the General Assembly of the Colony of New-York. Began the 8th Day of November, 1743; and Ended the 23d of December, 1765,* vol. 2. New York: Published by Order of the General Assembly, 1766.

New York Historical Society. *The Colden Letter Books,* vol. 1. 1760–1765, Collections of the New York Historical Society, vol. 9. New York: Printed for the Society, 1877.

———. *The Colden Letter Books,* vol. 2. 1765–1775, Collections of the NYHS, vol. 10. New York: Printed for the Society, 1878.

Nicolson, Colin, ed. *The Papers of Francis Bernard: Governor of Colonial Massachusetts, 1760-1769*, vol. 1: 1759-1763, Colonial Society of Massachusetts, vol. 73. Boston: The Society, 2007.

———. *The Papers of Francis Bernard: Governor of Colonial Massachusetts, 1760–1769*, vol. 2: 1764–1765, Colonial Society of Massachusetts, vol. 81. Boston: The Society, 2012.

———. *The Papers of Francis Bernard: Governor of Colonial Massachusetts, 1760-1769*, vol. 3: 1766-1767, Colonial Society of Massachusetts, vol. 83. Boston: The Society, 2013.

———. *The Papers of Francis Bernard: Governor of Colonial Massachusetts, 1760-1769*, vol. 4: 1768, Colonial Society of Massachusetts, vol. 86. Boston: Colonial Society of Massachusetts, 2015.

O'Callaghan, E. B., ed. *Documents relative to the colonial history of the State of New-York; procured in Holland, England, and France,* vol. 7. Albany: New York State Legislature, 1856.

Pickering, Danby. *The Statutes at Large, from Magna Charta to the end of the Eleventh Parliament of Great Britain, Anno 1761,* vol. 26. Cambridge, UK: Printed by Joseph Bentham, 1764.

———. *The Statutes at Large, from Magna Charta to the end of the Eleventh Parliament of Great Britain, Anno 1761,* vol. 27. Cambridge, UK: John Archdeacon, 1767.

Pitkin, Timothy. *A Political and Civil History of the United States of America, from the year 1763 to the Close of the Administration of President Washington,* vol. 1. New Haven, CT: Hezekiah Howe, 1828.

Ramsay, David. *The History of the American Revolution,* vol. 1. Philadelphia: R. Aitken and Son, 1789.

Reese, George, ed. *The Official Papers of Francis Fauquier Lieutenant Governor of Virginia, 1758-1768,* vol. 2. 1761-1763, Virginia Historical Society Documents, vol. 15. Charlottesville: University Press of Virginia, 1981.

——. *The Official Papers of Francis Fauquier Lieutenant Governor of Virginia, 1758-1768,* vol. 3: 1764-1768, Virginia Historical Society Documents, vol. 16. Charlottesville: University Press of Virginia, 1983.

Ritcheson, Charles R. "The Preparation of the Stamp Act," *The William and Mary Quarterly* 10, no. 4. 1953.

——. *British Politics and the American Revolution.* Norman: University of Oklahoma Press, 1954.

Russell, Lord John. *Correspondence of John, Fourth Duke of Bedford,* vol. 3. London: Longman, Brown, et al., 1846.

Saunders, William L., ed. *The Colonial Records of North Carolina,* vol. 6: 1759-1765. Raleigh: Joseph Daniels, 1888.

Schlesinger, Arthur M. *The Colonial Merchants and the American Revolution, 1763-1766.* New York: Columbia University, 1918.

——. *Prelude to Independence, the Newspaper War on Britain, 1764-1776.* New York: Knopf, 1958.

Scull, G. D., ed. *The Montresor Journals,* Collections of the New York Historical Society for the Year 1881, vol. 14. New York: The Society, 1882.

Shumate, Ken. *1764: The First Year of the American Revolution.* Yardley, PA: Westholme Publishing, 2021.

——. *The Sugar Act and the American Revolution.* Yardley, PA: Westholme Publishing, 2023.

Simmons, R. C. and P. D. G. Thomas, eds. *Proceedings and Debates of the British Parliaments Respecting North America, 1754-1783,* vol. 1, 1754-1764. Millwood, NY: Kraus International, 1982.

——. *Proceedings and Debates of the British Parliaments Respecting North America, 1754-1783,* vol. 2, 1765-1768. Millwood, NY: Kraus International, 1983.

——. *Proceedings and Debates of the British Parliaments Respecting North America, 1754-1783,* vol. 3, 1768-1773. Millwood, NY: Kraus International, 1984.

———. *Proceedings and Debates of the British Parliaments Respecting North America, 1754-1783*, vol. 4, Jan-May 1774. White Plains, NY: Kraus International, 1985.

Smith, William James, ed. *The Grenville papers: being the correspondence of Richard Grenville, earl Temple, K.G., and the right Hon. George Grenville, their friends and contemporaries*, vol. 2. London: John Murray, 1852.

Sosin, Jack M. *Agents and Merchants: British Colonial Policy and the Origins of the American Revolution, 1763-1775*. Lincoln: University of Nebraska Press, 1965.

Stamp Act Congress. *Proceedings of the Congress at New York*. Annapolis, MD: Printed by Jonas Green, 1766.

Story, Joseph. *Commentaries on the Constitution of the United States,* vol. 1. Boston: Hilliard, Gray, and Company, 1833, 133.

Stout, Neil R., ed. "The Missing Temple-Whately Papers," *Proceedings of the Massachusetts Historical Society,* third ser, vol. 104. 1992.

Strahan, William. "Correspondence between William Strahan and David Hall, 1763-1777. Continued." *PMHB* 10, no. 2. 1886.

Sutherland, Lucy S. "Edmund Burke and the First Rockingham Ministry," *EHR* 47, no. 185. 1932.

Thomas, P. D. G. *British Politics and the Stamp Act Crisis: The First Phase of the American Revolution, 1763-1767*. Oxford: Clarendon Press, 1975.

———. *Revolution in America: Britain and the Colonies, 1763–1776*. Cardiff: University of Wales Press, 1992.

Tyler, John W. and Elizabeth Dubrulle, eds. *The Correspondence of Thomas Hutchinson,* vol. 1: 1740-1766, Colonial Society of Massachusetts, vol. 84. Boston: The Society, 2014.

Ubbelohde, Carl. *The Vice-Admiralty Courts and the American Revolution*. Chapel Hill: University of North Carolina Press, 1960.

Virginia Historical Society. "Virginia Legislative Documents, continued," The *Virginia Magazine of History and Biography, VMHB*, vol. 10, no. 1. July 1902.

Weslager, Clinton Alfred. *The Stamp Act Congress: With an Exact Copy of the Complete Journal.* Newark: University of Delaware Press, 1976.

Wickwire, Franklin B. *British Subministers and Colonial America, 1763-1783*. Princeton, NJ: Princeton University Press, 1966.

Wood, Gordon S. *The American Revolution: A History*. New York: Modern Library, 2002.

Wood, Gordon S. ed. *The American Revolution: Writings from the Pamphlet Debate 1764–1772*, vol. 1. New York: The Library of America, 2015.

INDEX